THE WORDS OF A POET THAT WORE A STAR

By Kevin D. Lieby

ISBN:
ISBN-:13:

The Author-on himself, and Dedicatory

I was born to a railroad family in the Reno, Nevada area. It remains my hometown. My parents and both grandparents worked on the rails. Except for a two-year mission for The Church of Jesus Christ of Latter-Day Saints and three years in the US Army (1971-1974), that has been where I've lived.

I went to Sparks, Nevada schools, and attended the University of Nevada class of 1978. From 1975 to 2007, I was with the Washoe County Sheriff's Office.

I began writing poetry in 1969 when I met Blanche Fralic, the editor/publisher of "The Bluenose Rambler" in Western Shores, Lunenbury County, Nova Scotia, Canada while serving as a missionary. I submitted poems to her for three or four year while I continued my missionary service and then my Army service.

I continued writing. I participated in local open mike events, writer's workshops, and literary endeavors. These events and workshops include Inversely Poetic, Barnes and Noble Writer's Workshop, and various writing groups.

I made it a practice to support my fellow Deputies and Staff by writing poems commemorating those who lost their lives or took their lives while in service of the Sheriff and County, as life's pressures and experiences take a heavy toll on the minds and bodies of the Sword. I also memorialized retirements for some who touched my heart and made a mark in their careers there.

Enjoy reading the words of my pens, those snapshots of events and moments I've chosen to record. Pause on those over those who have passed. Their poems are a catharsis as I worked through my mourning. Enjoy my poems on writing of writing. I've included some assignments from writing workshops: a scene, a script, a story.

Contents

A Driving Rain

The ink black road stretches
        Into the heavy rain
Showing only the stripes
        That mark the lane.
And the windshield wipers,
        Like a metronome,
Steadily wipes the water
        As we travel to our home.
The tires splashing puddles
        That pool in the road
But keeping lots of traction,
        Our family's quite a load.
The noisy little droplets
        Patter on our car's roof
Making quite a racket.
        I'm glad it's waterproof.
We're passing mighty diesels
        throwing sheets of spray
Almost like the car wash
        I used just yesterday.
It surely makes me wonder
        If one of Nature's laws
Makes a storm cloud magnet,
        A great downpour to cause.
I can barely see the headlights
        They bounce out instead of back,
Instead of seeing white and gray
        I just see mostly black.
But I've always love rain driving
        Especially late at night
When you feel a blankets closeness
        and traffic's slow and light.

11/11/2002

A PRETTY PICTURE

Green trees against the blue-green grass.
  Yellow flowers in the meadow.
A pond that's like a glistening glass.
  A cabin in the hollow.

The steam that's running just below,
  The mountains to the right.
Through all these things I seem to know.
  This world is out of sight!

1968

A FALLEN STAR

By Kevin Lieby

a tribute to Keith Hasimoto

As a comet passes overhead
A star falls from the sky.
Not shapeless as a rock
But seven points catch the eye.
Not a star of cold metal
But a star of golden hue
With a meaning and a purpose
To prove what it could do.
But a symbol of the star
Affixed high upon his chest
Makes him different from the others,
Sets him apart from the rest.
It's a marker of pride, symbol of power
upon a strong and heaving breast.
But this time he reminds us
That we are the mortal kind
Until our time passes from us
And we at last all find
That we have but a short time
In our short swift flight from birth.
That we too must pass away.
A star fallen to the Earth.
Too often we feel we're invincible,
That armor and steel are strong.
But we're reminded by these times
That we might once be wrong,
That we aren't exceptions in life,
That for us it surely stops.
That the ticking, the constant ticking,
Is but from a fragile clock.
Bow your head, a star has fallen,
At half-mast the flags are flown
A black band crosses our stars
For we send a brother home.
The car lights tell the story
And we want the story known.
Bow your head, a star has fallen.
Can you hear the bugles drone?

A FATHER'S JOY

There comes a moment of awakening in the life of a blessed father
When he looks upon his progeny, on his grown sons and daughters,
And sees them not as children, as he remembers that once were.
But as independent men and women, so smart, so brave, so assure,
That he wonders when it happened, when they found themselves matured,
He thought that he had been watching for they'd been in his care.
And he should have noticed sooner, all the signs were pointing there.
Now he looks on them with pride. It swells his old heart.
They're doing the things he'd wished he'd done if he'd had the time to start.
His time has passed. He's gotten old. And they're so far apart.
And yet he sees himself in them, in the things they do and say.
The way they walk, and smile, their way with words, their interplay.
His DNA shows out in them. They mirror his genes and mind.
They remind him of his mother, of his father, many ways they define.
He flashes back to prior years when he'd done it just that way.
The way he'd held his own hands, he remembered, "back in the day".
It seems they learned so much more, they've had things he didn't have.
Electric things that just weren't there, the net, the phones, the pads.
His pads were bound in paper. His phone had dials and lines.
Our memory was in pen and ink. It all came out just fine.
They've gone to ways like he had, and gone to work and school.
They've learned to drive and sing and write poems, that's so cool.
They got that from their dad with their love of books and reading.
He no longer worries if they'll do right. They've already shown they can.
Now's his time to settle back and hold his grandkids tight.
He's done his job. He's shown the way. Now he's basking in their light.

05-20-2012

A FLOWING PEN

Sometimes I feel I can paint on paper
Using words flowing from a special pen.
Special because it fits in my big hands
And its ink flows smoothly from its tip.
It feels like a brush coloring canvas
But I don't have to dip it again and again,
Just print away making letters line up,
The ball rolling smoothly into lines, bit by bit
The words seem to come from the pen,
Oozing on to the paper like they were there
Just ready to stain the smooth surface
Of the sheet they were hiding under
The pressure of the pen brings them out,
Mysteriously appearing as if from thin air,
Produced by the Mage or the Muse
In a prodigious flash of light and wonder.
Still, it takes some talent to push the pen
And bring the poem to the light of day,
Sitting up in the dark of night
To give it time to show its true self.
Giving it a chance to surprise the poet
As it graces with black and gray
The surface of his empty book
He happened to just pull off his shelf
4/27/2009

WEIGHTY READING

Some people think that they're literate
If they just take a book and sit a bit.
But a much better gauge
Is in the words of a sage.
It is the weight of a book
Not the weight of it.

A SIERRA CHRISTMAS

A Sierra Christmas is a special thing
    To folks who live on deserts high
We too have carols, and bells that ring
    And tales of raindeer that can fly.

But the pinion is clothed in green and white
    And white tufted sage is held low by snow.
Coyotes howl at the moon so bright
    And the crisp clear air gives cheeks a glow.

Families close to the fire so warm,
    The smell of turkey, yams, and cakes.
The strings of cranberries, tinsel, and popcorn,
    And balls that babies grab and break.

Gifts are wrapped in paper so bright
    With colors gold, and red, and green,
And foil reflects the stars and light
    All fitly around our manger scene.

A SON RETURNS

You send a boy out
To do the work of a man
And he comes back a man
For there is a spirit
That seeks to grow large,
The way it should and can.
Especially when it's in the service
Of our God. He's grown
In body and in spirit
Forging a heart of steel
In the testimony of faith
With service he can't forget.
He went to a land
We have only read about
And heard of in the news
And we came to miss him,
Though the years flew fast
Till his return came due.
So he came back with honor.
We saw he had grown
As one sent forth does.
And now he stands before us
As he did once before
Yet there is more here
Than there was last time
And we bid him welcome.
Our arms drawing him near.
For as a son he has
But done the Father's bidding
As we have been shown
When another Son was sent
To live, to die, and rise,
Yet made His message known
As our example to follow.
In our own small ways
To follow Him, our Savior,
To spread our arms open
To the world with like message
He left us to deliver.
And this young man will go on
To serve in other calls
For there is also work here.
For the work of faith ends
Only when the trumpet sounds
For the Son to reappear.

04-21-1999

ADAM

Adam, Thou Ancient One,
      The first of men on earth
Came here to give all men a chance
      To have a mortal birth.
To come to earth without a mom
      To start a family
With Eve, thy wife, you did it all
      That man could even be.
You led the way,
      Through ways, so far, untrod
You led on trails not marked
      Back to our Lord, Our God.
With Abel and Cain, then with Seth,
      You begat the royal line
To start this race of men on earth
      That's lasted till our time.
You took the charge, good or bad,
      With nothing but your hands
Then shaped the world and made it grow
      Into kingdoms, fifes and lands.
Neigh a thousand years you stayed the course
      Until your time had come
To pass the keys to your children dear
      And return from whence you'd come.
The Veil you'd passed, you passed again
      And received your heavenly crown.
With Eve to reign there at your side
      Her name of great renown
A help meet walking hand in hand
      At your side she'll ever be,
From Eden you had both walked forth
      Into all eternity.

06/16/2004

Alone again

Alone again, without love or light,
    No friend but a remote control
The book light and the radio
    Trying to fill the void in my soul.
Eating just for something to do,
    Working as a way to pass the time,
Writing to see if feelings are there,
    Twisting words and thoughts into a rhyme.
I only wanted to feel alone again
    When they shoveled dirt down on my face.
But here I am in a one room apartment
    Trying to find both my rhythm and my pace.
I feel the weight of Captain Kirk's fate,
    To face the end alone, not sharing, not caring,
Just doing what needs to be done,
    Turning away from others, the web of life tearing.
I never worked to live apart and alone
    But I just guess it was meant to be
Because that's how it always ends up,
    Pushed away and allowed to drift to sea.

11-23-11

As a Friend lay dying

In memory of Larry Collins

We go to work day after day
As a friend lay stricken and weak
Brought down by the cancer within him
As his life had reached its peak.

We're better for having known him.
We've known him long and well.
We'll miss him by our side each day
And the tales of him we'll tell.

Some remember him thirty years ago
When he shared our badge and task
All uniformed in County green
Booking crooks in times now past.

The old jail was our common haunt
And we dumped a crook or two
Together we would walk the tiers
And share the things we knew.

Then for years our ways were parted
Though we saw each other oft
And we never lost our kinship
As our paths have often crossed.

Now you've gone a long way off
And crossed that one way veil
And rowed with Charon the river Styx
At who's very thought we pale.

We'll miss you, our old good friend,
We'll no more see your face.
Unless we meet you over there
Blessed by hope and Grace.

07/13/2005

ASHES

She cradles in her arms a silver urn
As she rocks herself to sleep.
And it holds the ashes of one she loves
That she's chosen to keep.
It soothes her heart and calms her mind
And allows that sleep to come.
She aches to rest and yearns for food
But her body would have none.
With his ashes here she finds her breath
And the calm she really needs
And her children sleep but fitfully
Like the windblown autumn leaves.
They had good days in former years
As they raised the girls in peace.
But the stress of war had worn him down
And he could not find release.
And now she clutches ashes to her breast
And she struggles for relief
For his time's now past into memory
Of a life too short and brief.

07-24-2013

AXIOM FOR WRITERS

Without dreams you're hollow
    Like a chocolate Easter bunny
You're either full of marshmallow
    Or air, It's cloudy or sunny.

My axiom, or should I say our axiom, explains the soul of a writer.

Writers have dreams... The Great American Novel, a prize winning poem,
The Nobel prize for literature... If we didn't have a dream we wouldn't, couldn't write.

If you didn't have a dream what would you write about???

Fiction writers put a dream on paper. Their pens leak dreams onto paper for a novel is but a dream in print.

Poets dream in verse. Poets bleed their dreams and bare their souls onto the paper of life. They paint with words with all the colors of the language. The pallet of a poet is the language. The pen, his brush, scribes upon the canvas his dreams.

The non-fiction writer dreams the dreams of another. He documents on paper the lives of those who have lived their dreams. Our history is the scriblings of a writer dreaming of the laurels of the world. To be recognized as an authority on the dreams of another.

Without dreams what would we write??
Is this what a writers block is, The lapse of a dream??

Is our work but a waking dream at our typewriter, our computer, or our pad of paper??

Machinations of Imagination is trade. Putting our dreams into words and stringing them along into hours of dreams for the minds of others to share.

We write so others may feel what we felt when our dream flowed from our pens onto the dried pulp of our pads. We are saying, "Share my dreams with me. Look I'm not hollow. I'm full of dreams that I can express well enough that you can find my dreams in your mind too.
See, I'm not full of air. I'm full of a cream skimmed from the top of life."

Bah, Humbug, Valentine

I loved a woman yesterday.
At least I thought I did
But she told me I was wrong.
I guess only women understand.

She would be my valentine
If like the tin man
She only had a heart.
Maybe that is the secret.
Love is an acting game
That is used against men
To force them to feel
That only women can really love.

But I've seen that cold hard lump
That you call a heart
And it runs at the L-Word
Or just its mere mention.
But you tell us it's our fault
And you know you lie.
A woman wants a slave
That does what she tells him.
Not a lover with a mind.
Maybe that's why poets
Say that love is crazy,
That a man is mad with love,
That he is head over heals
For the love of a woman.

When the woman herself cannot love
Because she has been taught
By yet other women that they
Are in charge of the world.

So we buy valentines
And big hearts full of chocolates
To show you what?
That we will waste hours of work
Just to throw it away in meaningless,
Yes, meaningless displays of goods.

Like we would even remember
The day if you didn't have reminders
All over the papers about it.
Men don't even read those ads.
Women shop, Men buy.
And there it is. We buy you.
We show we care by money.
It comes down to the dollar,
The rose, the gold, and the diamond.

Men wouldn't even talk to you
If it wasn't for testosterone.
Nature drives a man to you
Like salmon's drive to spawn.
But unlike the salmon
It is not the last, breathing act.
Men keep coming back for more.
And therein lies the secret.
A man's drive can never be fulfilled
Except for just a fleeting moment
Then the urge again builds
Twisting his brain into servitude
To the focus of that drive.

Maybe like the salmon he does die
At least as a separate person.
He is no longer master of himself.
He is like that salmon on the shore
Breathing air that cannot reach his blood.

But he breathes faster and faster
In a futile attempt to survive.
But nature is against him too.

I want to breathe hard and fast
And nibble on that slim neck
Until you moan and breathe hard.
But that is just testosterone talk.

I want to be valued, not wanted.
I want to spend years gazing
Into those eyes of yours
Without feeling chains about me,
Without feeling forced to perform,
Without being forced to pay,
For what you tell us is freely given.
Ya, Sure, Like that's the truth.
I have seen the truth.
The truth is a leach
Sucking the life out of men
And leaving a hollow shell
Where a man's soul was.

See, Here's a valentine.
I'm giving you my heart
So you can slam it to the floor
And stomp it to a pulp.
And then you will be like
All the others I tried to trust.
My heart isn't hard.
It's covered with scars and prints
Of the boots of those I tried to love.
See, those latest prints are yours.

02/10/2002

BEYOND THAT DOOR

A Poem for Deputy ROSS

Once more the Highland Pipes and toll of bell
   Reminds us why the flags are short their staffs
And why these stars are crossed with black and tell
   Of another of our brothers whose time has passed.

A locker free of its burden no longer holds secure
   The garb and martial tools he once carried proud.
His shield graces not his breast nor medals shining pure
   Attest that he had earned far better than a shroud.

With heavy hearts and furrowed brow we come to bid
  A friend and colleague fond adieu and see him depart
This fleeting world of measured time to one instead
   Where time marks not its pace in beating of a heart.

What matters Time when you pass the portals of the gate
   Where Peter's sainted post stands with pearls covered fine
Bids welcome to our missing friend. Who was but late
   Sharing time with us right here, checking cells and fighting crime

He did his part not knowing he would be called so soon
   To leave the mortal world behind and "go on before"
Where we can but hope to be found in tune
   When we are called to follow him beyond that door.

09-29-99

BIG JOHN FEROAH

Big John Feroah has reached
That time
When he can finally hit
The door
And leave the job of
Fighting crime
'Cause he's old and deaf
And sore.
No longer will he grace
The halls
As he has for all
These years.
No more will all our
Shoulders hurt
From his blows, to us,
His peers
We'll miss this giant of
A man,
He's been a good and
Faithful friend.
He's had his moments in
The sun
But the work has got
To end.

His legends here are cut
In stone,
But Admin. won't let them
Be told-
Seems there is a statute
Of limitations
Or just a copyright that
Needs sold.
We'll get together and swap
Some yarns
When we all get away
From here.
It may well be over
A dinner.
It could well be over
A beer.
It's been good and it's
Been fun,
And it's been a damn
Long haul.
Big John's had enough of
County work.
He's now at the lake
Or Mall.

10/10/2003

Blood on the pavement

Blood on the pavement
Looks black at night.
You can tell from the sheen
That it's fresh
And it flowed from the wounds
Now bound tight
From a cop with a wound
In his chest.

It's lit by the flicker
Of lights, red and blue
That comes from the
Black and whites.
The color of those
That bleed for you
In the presence or
Absence of lights.

The heat of the fight
For life or death.
The burn of the metal
Called lead.
The flash of the muzzle,
Its fiery breath
Puts both men in a
Hospital bed.

One bound for the glory
Of a purple heart.
Valor hanging from his
Pocket and chest.
Treated as a hero
From the start
His picture on the wall
With the best.

The other bound
For a life in a cell
Till he dies there,

A broken old man.
Then his soul goes
Directly to hell
And you can bury his
Ash in a can.

The brave hearted man
Will get up again
And strap on his
Armor and gun
And get back to work
Shipping crooks to the pen
And travel the streets
Till he's done.

We'll welcome him back
In a few precious weeks
When he's better and
Out of the rack,
And he's ready for action
With just a few tweaks
And he's out there
Leading the pack.

He's been there before,
Leading the fight,
With a badge polished
Bright on his chest.
He'll be there once more
Doing what's right
Where the heat of the
Battle is pressed.

You're in all our prayers
Till you heal up
And stand by our side
On the line.
We'll set you a place
And fill up your cup
And toast you awaiting
That time.

To our wounded friend Al   08/22/2007

Bookworm's Lament

I've been to a hundred lands
And a thousand cities,
Across the sky, and space, and time.
I've witnessed history being made.
I've seen the future and the past.
I've been the first, the current, the last,
The best, the worst, the crass.
I've seen through his eyes,
My eyes, her eyes, its eyes.
I've seen war and peace,
Love and hate and crime.
I've been warm and cold,
Wet and dry, and young and old.
I've heard rhyme and oration,
Soliloquy and bravado,
The cries of an army's charge,
And the cooing of a dove.
I've questioned "who done it?"
And have seen the smoking gun
On the dark and stormy night
Or under the blazing sun.
I've read Holy Words
Sent forth from God
And seen His wisdom
And felt His rod.
I've explored the mysteries of the Tao,
And the quotes from master Kung.
My reading list is never done.
My old book bag must weigh a ton.
Mount a booklight on my grave,
Or run a drop light in my cave,
All I want to do is read.
I'll just decay to bookworm feed.

02/11/2004

BRASS PLATES

Brass plates mounted row by row
            Bearing names of those we know
Mounted on a cold hard wall
            Each plate marks a Hero's fall.

Men who chose to make a stand
            to uphold laws of the land.
Men who stood and were cut down,
            Spilled their blood upon the ground.

This has made this Hallowed earth,
            Sacred and priceless is its worth.
Doff thy hats in humble prayer
            In memory of those listed there.

Brass plates mounted row by row
            Bearing names of those we know.
Mounted on a cold hard wall
            Each plate marks a Hero's fall.

07/96

BYTES...

My life is controlled by bytes,
    The hard drive spins my future,
The mouse points my way
    Into the brains of my computer.
The great seventeen inch eye
    Stares back into my mind
Sharing with me my poems.
    In its memory it can find
The deep things of my heart
    Which I have often shared
Most readily in the dark
    When into it I've stared
And prattled into its keyboard
    The musings of my soul
Until my wrists tweak with pain.
    Upon me it takes its toll.
Yet on it I must tarry
    While It still gives off light
It keeps me peaceful company
    Often far into the night.
For on it I discover
    That which most men hide.
The poems deep inside me
    Buried 'neath this crusty hide.
Come to me my muses
    Stir poems from my soul
And type them on this keyboard
    For poems make me whole.
I like them set in verses.
    I like them all to rhyme.
I want to read them to the world
    If you just grant me time.
Again I type into the night
    The room lit with your glow
Feel the verse upon your keys
    And feel the muses flow.

07-09-2001

Chocolate as a Basic Food Group.

Most people who know me know that I consider chocolate to be more than just one of the basic food groups.

It is obviously vegetable. It is made from beans (coca)and sugar (beats or cane). But it is also dairy. They even call it milk chocolate. It can be poured as a syrup over Ice Cream. It can be mixed into ice-cream as flavoring, chips, or syrup. It can be mixed into warm milk for hot chocolate.

It can be mixed with grains (Toll House cookies, Crunch bars, cakes, doughnuts, brownies).

It can be mixed with Nuts (bridge mix, Peanut clusters, almond clusters, cashew clusters). It can cover berries and fruit (Cherries, raisins, Blue berries, Cranberries, dates, bananas, apples). It can cover candy treats (truffles, nougats, mints). It can cover insects (Ants and grasshoppers).

It can be eaten plain in any of a hundred of processed flavors, shapes, and serving sizes. It can be powdered, creamed, flaked, shaved, brewed, cast, dropped, broken, swirled, whipped, melted, blended, coated or liquored. It can assume any form or combine with almost any flavor.

You might say it is the most versatile of the foods used by mankind, or womankind or in the case of my cocker spaniel Canine kind. His favorite food was oreos and the last food he ate was a Chocolate Sandwich Cookie. I knew his time had come when he turned his nose up to chocolate.
They published a medical paper a year ago that told me that chocolate was good for your health. It also said that the more you eat the longer and happier you would live. This is one study I took seriously. At my present rate of consumption I should live forever.
But most important when dealing with chocolate is that some consider f things that the Food and Drug Administration is outlawing because of their addicting qualities, Chocolate may come under its heavy hand.
Can you imagine, especially near Christmas time, having to get a prescription for Chocolate.
I think a person could suffer dangerous withdrawals if left without the medicinal properties of chocolate to soothe the mad craving of the addict.
Put the chocolate down, back slowly away and no one will get hurt.

12-11-01

CHOCOLATE

Millennia ago our wise leaders codified prohibitions outlawing those acts and objects that would sway or detract us from a single minded devotion to the One True God. Those acts or objects so proscribed by these codes are referred to as sins.

In this day and age a marvelous thing has arisen that may fill the above definition as something that is able to sway even the heart and soul of the most devout believer from his single-minded devotion to his Heavenly Benefactor.

This insidious concoction is produced from the roasted seed of a tree first harvested by the Nahuatl tribe of South America. As powder, as paste, as syrup, or formed as a bar it is mixed with soluble crystalline carbohydrates and the secretions from the mammary glands of the genus Bos, which are domesticated and nurtured for the collection of this fluid.

The oils and liqueur of this concoction are blended and roasted and cooked and molded into items of veneration whose consumption by members of the human race sends the consuming addict into a sensual, almost concupiscent ecstasy, And then a compulsion to consume copious amounts of the compound. This obsession commonly leading to an increasing of bodily mass and the resultant lowering of self-esteem that can be temporarily overcome by again ingesting the concoction again and again and again.

In every mall in America there seems to be shops whose sole purpose is to enslave unsuspecting shoppers into the wanton consumption of this chemically altered seed extract.

Surely, If this substance had been in production in the area of the Holy Land when Father Abraham and Moses were receiving directions from the Unnamed God of the desert another line would have been inscribed by the hand of that God upon the tablets brought down from the mount.

"Thou shalt not consume Chocolate."
"See's and desist"

11-22-1999

Christmas 2002

It's music that puts Christ in my Christmas,
The hymns and the songs of His birth,
Of wise men and shepherds that seek Him,
And the promise of peace here on earth.

It's not just the presents that I'm given
Or the lights shining bright on the tree
But the lights in eyes of the children
That brings the Spirit of Christmas to me.

All the calls we receive from our family
That cannot be with us this year,
They remind us of good times together
And may bring both a laugh and a tear.

Can you pause, just a moment, this Christmas
And ponder the things that you love
And remember the gift we were given
Of a Son sent to us from above?

12/25/2002

CLEAN UP

Dark blue is the sky.
   The sun has gone down.
The evening is so quiet.
   The stars form a crown.
I think in the stillness
   Of the wonders of God
When He formed the sky,
   The sea, the sod.
And filled them with wonders
   Which startle the mind
If you will but look
   And see what you'll find.
I know this sound simple
   But look at His deeds
And just what He's provided,
   Each and everyone's needs.
He's provided all these wonders,
   Every plant, snake, and bird
And all that they dwell in
   And the ink in this word
And the ground we walk on
   The air which we use
But look what has happened!!
   All the things we abuse.
We pollute all the water
   The air is all smog
Each and every great forest
   We burn and we log.
Oh tell me what happens
   In a few short-lived years
When nothing can live here.
   Yes, These are my fears.
Oh man will you wise up
   And see what you've done
You've ruined most everything
   That is under the sun.
Why don't you clean up
   And care for this place
Because if you don't
   We'll smell up all space.

1970

CONTEMPLATION OF BEAUTY

Have you ever watched a campfire
As the flame rises from the coals?
Have you ever watched the moon rise
Over black and silver knolls?
Have you ever watched the other sights
That touch deep within your souls?
Have you ever beheld God’s beauty
In the way the waves do roll?

Many of us don’t stop to think
Of this beauty all around,
That ranges from the tallest trees
To the fertile grassy ground.
I say to you, “Stop a while
And see the thing I’ve found.
Just by taking a few minutes,
Just relaxing, and setting down.”

1970

A COMING CHRISTMAS

The wind builds the snow up against the west side of my house.
The chill factor is so low it makes your fingers numb.
But people are already putting up the twinkling lights
That tell us that the holiday season has come.

The smell of wood burning carries on the breeze in the morning
And the odors of pine and gingerbread spice up the old living room.
In my house the smells are likely to come from a can
But still brings back the memories of days gone too soon.

There are so many glossy and colorful ads in the paper
That it makes them impossible to burn
And if you leave them within reach of the kids
You will find hints for gifts at every turn.

Everyone has their hands out for your money.
Every charity sends you a donation envelope
In case you have any money left in your pocket
Though that seems about a fruitless hope.

Put away that brown and orange decor.
The stores didn't even wait for Halloween
To get over before they started putting out
Rows and rows of basic red and green.

It seems the television shows get shorter
So they can have more of those commercials
That tell us what to buy and where to buy it
From clothes to food, from toys to vehicles.

But I, myself, am just praying for peace
That those guns could be silent again,
That the sounds in the night will be carolers
Singing of good news coming forth unto men.

11-26-2001

CONJUGATION OF A DREAM

I have a dream.
      You have a dream.
            We all have dreams.
                  Whatever that means.
I want my dreams.
      You want your dreams.
            We want our dreams.
                  If we only had the means.
But I dream alone,
      And you dream alone.
            And we all dream alone
                  Under the sky's dark dome.
I have time for dreams.
      You have time for dreams.
            We have time for dreams
                  Or so it seems.
My dreams make me work.
      Your dreams make me work.
            Our dreams make us work
                  For a boss that's a jerk.
I need to close my eyes.
      You need to close your eyes.
            We need to close our eyes
                  To dreams, alone, the dream dies.

10-11-2001

CRUSHED CRICKETS

The crunching sounds of crushing crickets/ Rises from the tires of my cougar/ As I slowly wend my way homeward/ Inside the comfort of my car.

Like an infantry's rapid advance/ The crickets rush across the road/ To be mowed down by the weight/ Of my wheel's heavy load.

No longer can they forage unimpeded/ Across this valley's floor/ As they've done here for millennia/ In the time we call "before".

And now they chew upon our lawns,/ Our bushes and our trees,/ And we curse them like the Mormons did/ As they're eating all the leaves.

I'd read of it in papers/ But now it's all around/ You can see the darn things moving/ And they're covering the ground.

Should we pray again for seagulls/ To munch upon their prey?/ Should we spray them and bait them/ As they feast upon our hay?

Look, they're up there on the building./ Look, they're down there on the floor./ They seem to be most everywhere./ Are they munching on the door?

Can they eat right through the wallboard,/ Consume the hardwood floor?/ Or grow to giant monsters/ As we find in tales of yore?

Aren't the darn things big enough?/ They're nearly three inches long./ Then the darn things run away/ When you mow them with your lawn.

Then here comes those darn cicada./ They make the bushes buzz./ They look like big old houseflies./ No telling what each does.

They both make summer interesting,/ If you jump at things that move./ If either of them land on you,/ They can put you off your groove.

But summer only lasts a while,/ There will soon enough be snow,/ And long before that get to us,/ they'll find their place to go.

So now we wait, some patiently,/ Till the darn things go away./ Until then I'll just play inside./ It's cooler there anyway.

07/11/2002

Dawn of love

As I sit here in early morning
      And see the sun's almost to rise
I contemplate the beauty of you;
      The feelings when I gaze in your eyes.

I feel the closeness of our hearts
      And the joy within our souls
More beautiful than the sun rise
      As it rises from the knolls.

Based not on the momentary pleasures
      But in the appreciation of the future.
A love, not a flash of pleasure,
      But a love we can nurture.

A love that can grow forever greater
      Expanding to the fullness of life
Never to be separated by death,
      Neither by trials nor by strife.

I cannot envision a greater love
      With fullness and consideration of all
Growing as ours does right now
      Built on a foundation that cannot fall.

This is what I think of now
      And the sun is now shining bright.
In the sky it shows forth brilliantly
      And truly is a beautiful sight.

I must carry on now, as does the sun,
      But my thoughts of you shall go on
For it is deep within my heart
      And more vibrant than the dawn.

DEATH

Death came close to me today
　　But it hasn't brought me sorrow.
I think we'd all be better off
　　If we all died tomorrow.

Some think that death is sad
　　Filled with sorrow of all kinds
The reason I think death's bad
　　Is that I am left behind.

Don't you think He's happy there
　　Somewhere across the veil
Where it is peaceful all the time
　　And on a cloud he sails.

I think death is a happy thing
　　About which we should all rejoice.
But we can make it happy or sad,
　　It's all in our own choice.

1970

Decorate

It took me ten minutes
to decorate
And it is because
I'm single.
A couple of my ornaments
Still hang
Where I left them hanging
last year.
In this I do not
Exaggerate
Just plug it in see
It twinkle.
Being alone I don't give
a dang.
Who would know if I left
It here?
My Christmas dinner is on
One plate,
Freezer to microwave makes it
So simple
And last year it was
The same.
Maybe it's lucky you
Weren't near.

11-27-95

DEP. RIOS

"WHO IS IT!" No longer rumbles like thunder through the halls
Knocking inmates from their perches and spackle from the walls.
No longer will his nose be seen far sooner than the rest.
BILL RIOS is retiring......House One will lose the best.
Years and years of showing up each day an hour early
And slugging down some coffee with his cronies, acting surly.
Eating up someone else's treats, begging candy from the nurses.
The Kitchen may send ice-cream when they feel his coerces.
'EL PRESIDENTE' he was called when he sat upon the board
And he ran the Association like a "Spanish Overlord".
The Sheriff shook and quivered when Rios showed his power,
He knew he'd have to listen for hour after hour.
He'd argue sports for hours, even if you'd rather not
And it seemed to go forever when the Niners acted hot!
With him and Mike kibitzing of scores and field goals,
No pity if they fumbled one. They kept them on their toes.
But the jail will now be quiet. His badge they will retire.
His fifth wheel is now ready. His replacement set to hire.
You know we all will miss him, though some of us not much.
The inmates will be restless. They'll miss that RIOS touch

Written with love, Kevin
1999

DO NOT CRY FOR ME

Do not cry for me,
      One left behind by death.
One cries not for the leaf
      As it falls from the tree
But maybe for the forest
      Laid bare by the frost of winter,
For I have but been touched
      By the icy hand of time.
I shall not again be wakened up
      By the mornings light to labor
Beneath the warm sun of this land
      To warm and light this house
And keep food upon the table
      For those for whom I've cared.
Cared enough to drag this old shell
      From its warm welcome rest,
Too many times to count
      And sallied forth to make a coin
To throw upon someone's counter,
      Trading time for time for time
Until my shell lies cold and empty
      To be carried out like garbage
In a sack or box or can
      And placed beneath soil cold.
My heart beats ever within my words
            Left in the poems upon this pad
Never stilled while readers live.
            Reliving dreams and thoughts I've had.

12-24-2003

DOWNTIME

Last night I sat alone
      In front of that
            Brain sucking box
Entertained like a stone
      Mesmerized by nothing,
            Drained of life.
Vegging on my Lazyboy,
      Feet at Shoulder height,
            Airing my socks,
Munching on some leftovers
      Spinning my spaghetti
            Between fork and knife.

God! What a waste of time,
      Just doing nothing and
            Feeling a little guilty
'Cause I could be writing
      Poems in the quiet,
            Striving to create.
Why? Is it a crime
      Not to write?
            And feeling lazy.
Sometimes you need downtime
      Winding slowly down
            Until it's late.

04/11/2002

DREAM OF WEDLOCK

I dream of that coming day
     When we shall be together
     For we are now far apart.

When those words of love we say
     That can be equaled never,
     Welding deep within our hearts

I dream of you in white
     Standing at my side, enjoined
     Before the alter of love.

I see this wondrous sight
     As we are in wedlock joined
     Before our God, Who is above.

I look forward in Anxiousness
     To this time in the future
     But now it is far ahead

Growing closer by our faithfulness
     By which we nurture it
     Till those words are said.

1969

DREAMS OF YOU

My love, your blue eyes reach deep within me
Sending a thrill through me, touching my heart.
My love for you is growing up without bounds,
My heart is with you though we're apart.

Your picture reminds me of your beauty,
Of your eyes and the softness of your hair,
And I can hardly await the coming time
When I will be with you there.

Wait for me, you're my reason to live,
My reason to work, And breathe. and yearn.
For you I keep my thoughts in gentle train
To you my dearest thoughts will always turn.

1970

DREADED BEAUTY

I see the small inconspicuous bloom of the Dandelion
   Growing as it were in a field of rolling grasses;
And I, Having a few minutes to spend in contemplation,
   pluck it up, as I stroll along, as I pass.

Then setting on a nearby stump I study it,
   Trying to see the real beauty of the bloom;
This bloom of a dreaded weed, an unwanted castaway;
   What beauty is held within it, much I assume.

Yes; there is much beauty there, much, much beauty:
   The yellow symmetry of the flower first suppress you.
The smooth lines and fine edges in flawless form
   Going down, down until they finally slide from view.

The yellow is so brilliant and yet so soft
   And the green leaf-like base pieces accent it perfectly;
Put together, each piece flawless and so positioned
   That no artist could ever capture it so naturally.

Yes, it's a weed I'm talking of at this time,
   But as most things in this world often passed by.
But on this day, of all the days of my life,
   This weed's true beauty and wonder has caught my eye.

1969

DRUDGERY

We long for sleep.
 The toils of the day
  Rest heavy on our old bones.
Our eyes are heavy.
 They've been open too long
  And they long for sweet darkness.
But as is usual
 We have ventured far
  This day from our homes.
It will be hours
 Before we snuggle down
  And achieve our rest.

But such is life
 We pay our way each day
  By the work of our hands.
We fill our table
 By the hours we spend
  Chasing the long green.
We just work away
 Like some mindless drones
  Or some high-tech machines
We could just sleep
 And stay in bed all day,
  Just lay there and dream.

But that would mean
 No grub on the table tonight,
  No mugs to warm our hearts,
No books to read,
 No light to write by,
  No pens nor paper here.
So we get up

When the clock says we must
And our drudgery starts,
Not because we want,
But because we need,
And our needs come dear.

I roll this carcass
Out of my warm bed
Every dad gummed morning,
Then out I go
Into the crazy world
To squirrel away another buck
To pay my bills,
To put gas in the car,
To buy some good clothing.
The fruit of labor
Seems meager each week
When in your wallet you tuck

Some tattered green papers
That mean in the end
That you'll have to go back
Another week of work
To please some old fart
Who signs the pay check.
Then you're back again,
As sure as the sun shines
Warm upon your tired back,
To fill that timecard
To pay the bills.
Is it quitting time yet?

We live like others,
Enjoying our time after work
In rest or at play.
It's not the work

That we slave for
But the rest of the day
When we can do,
Not just what we're told,
But we have our own say
At what we do
And where we will go
As if we're fleeing away.

And fly we do,
To share rhymes with others,
To share our pain
Here by the river,
With those we call friends,
Because they're poets too.
And they also work,
But they also write poems
And they focus the blame
On why we labor,
Not just for the money
But what it has let us do.

So tomorrow we work
As we did this morning
And maybe so the day before.
Doing the work thing,
Chasing the long green,
Filling out the timecard.
We often show pleasure
And our time do we measure
Till we're going out the door
Until we make a killin'
Writing poems by the million
Like Milton or 'The Bard'

06/23/2001

Electronic Slaves

The airport is hot and noisy.
      The almost constant drone
Of the announcements equals
      The ubiquitous Cell Phone.
The constant interaction
      Of the seasoned traveler
Talking to his cell which
      Provides a constant banter.
We once could detect schitzoids
      By observing their behavior.
Now you must discover
      If a phone is in their ear.
Making personal phone calls
      In the privacy of the crowded
Passenger Seating Area is equivalent
      Of an exhibitionist exhibited,
Revealing his own private fantasy
      To an unwilling public.
We being an unwilling party
      To his privates (electronic).
And another sets there
      Plugging his laptop computer
Into the airport's outlet.
      Like a seasoned commuter
Not wasting his time
      While he awaits his connection.
Tapping away at his keyboard,
      Focusing all his attention
Late in the night
      On the dimly glowing screen
That must define his life,
      And maybe his dream.
Am I an electronic junkie too?
      Playing my color GameBoy.
Burning up some time
      On my electronic toy.
08/01/2002

EMOTIONS

Emotions are like tight wires
Ready to snap with strain
Any word could spark arguments
Like a spark starting a flame.

Fighting these emotions is hard
For the strain is increasing
Tightening its hold on us
Tightening, Tightening, never ceasing

We must work together though
To loose these tightening bands
To halter our own emotions
So we can be friends.

1971

The End Of A Star

For Deputy John Wiberg

Once again on dark streets
In the middle of night
On roads slick from storm
A star has lost light.

With screech of wet tires
And the crunching of steel
This light has gone out
Of "The Man" at the wheel.

He was off to the rescue
On some kind of call
He'd just got from Dispatch
This cop big and tall.

But now he's laid low
And no more gives breath
But passed through the veil
That non-poets call death

And his girls now morn
For their daddy's not here
And the widow sheds tears
That he's no longer near.

The friendship and the flowers
Are showered on them today
There'll be emptiness forever
Because he has gone away.

We all shed some tears,
We all hurt deep inside
Because he's not with us
Not here at our side.

Because he wore the star
On his chest with pride
And wore the same colors,
And gun on his side.

Now his flower draped casket
Makes us sober and sad.
We remember the good times
We had with this lad.

Wish we could tell him
Just how much he meant
To us gathered round him
During time we have spent.

Now they've folded his flag
And the bagpipe draws near,
The sound of the bugle
Sounding regal and clear.

We take a few moments
And salute him once more
We mark, "Out of Service"
And return to the war.

05-11-2004

ESSENTIAL OILS

Words, having no weight of their own,
Crush the soul from the hopeless poet
Rendering him into the essential oils
Of his own Immortality.
Driving him with the force
Of an inked quill
To scrawl out his blood
Upon the parchment of his own skin...
Stretched out upon the rack and pulled taught
By the ropes of his twisted mind.
Searching for its own meaning
In the world of the literary damned.

Words, falling in the night
As gentle as the snow upon the thirsty land
That melts to naught but salty sweat
Under the heat of the new day.
Words full of the pigments of his heart
Writhing upon the lines of his book
That only the blind will read
To make sense to the senseless readers.

Words, that only the poet can know
Ekes out their silence in the ears of the muses
To become crashing cymbals of what is meant
To be hidden in the heart.

Words etched in the open wounds
Left by the talons of a lost lover
Upon the back of the bleeding poet
Where he himself cannot see
The scars in their fury
Except in the mirror finish of his pen
As it bleeds upon the paper
Before him in the night
Lit by the flickering taper fueled
By the tallow rendered from his own essential oil.

04/26/2002

THE F-WORD

I get tired of hearing the F-word.
Some of you remind me of a two year old
Who has learned a new word that shocks his parents.
I want to shout "Get a life."

But I remember a time in my life
When I thought that it was
All that life was about myself.

Have you tried to be a poet?
To be able to write about love and not say
The F-word in every other line you write.

Have you tried to say it all
Without having to get into a description
Of the sticky details of a biological union?

Do you stop to realize
That the closeness and intimacy of sex
Is mostly in the minds of the participants?

To hold the one you care for closely
Without the barriers of cloth to separate
Your souls as you blend into one emotion.

To give all you can of yourself
To one who is giving all of their self
And exploding together in a moment of passion.
Then laying together, embracing,
Warm and damp like limp wash clothes
That have been wrung together and now are spent.

It’s more than a chase.
It should be more than the climax.
It should be precious, like a pearl,
Made up of layers and layers of precious moments
And growing in value day after day in your hearts.
Hidden from the encroaching world of humanity
That cannot share the closeness you both feel.

Open your minds to your hearts,
That’s what a poet is supposed to do.
Not simply the facts like a cop writing a report.

We don’t have just one word
That describes the act of passionate union.
We have a myriad of expressions that color,
And shade, and blend the emotions
Of that experience we treasure as Love.

To limit our vocabulary to the F-Word
Is in itself a rape of the human language.

Break out of that bondage,
Make your mind your sex organ
Because most of you are out of yours anyway
When you are experiencing it
As just
“the F-Word.”

01-14-2001

FATHER

Father ...---...
When I come to thee in prayer
Are you there?
Father ...---...
When the pains of life bring tears
Are you there?
Father ...---...
When life gives me naught but night
Are you there?
Father ...---...
When sore trials make me cry
Are you there?

Child -.-- . ...
I Am always here
To hear your prayer.
Child -.-- . ...
I Am always near
To dry your tear.
Child -.-- . ...
I Am your True Light
In darkest night.
Child -.-- . ...
I Am always nigh
To hear your cry.

B r o. L i e b y
-... .-. --- .-.. .. . -... -.-

Favorite time

This is my favorite time

Of the evening

When that Cloud hanging

Over the mountain

Has it's bottom burnt red

By the setting sun.

Then like the lights

Of a stage

Which can slowly

Fade to black

Clouds cool to gray

As day is done

08-31-99

FEELING MUSIC

Slow music drifts through my mind
And takes me to a quiet place,
I feel slowly moving water
And the sun on my face.
The volume increases and builds
And the drummer holds a beat
You can almost feel him swaying
Back and forth upon his seat.
The volume drops to pianissimo
From triple forte where it soared,
The music builds upon itself.
At least you can't get bored.
Now the beat is moving fast
Like a pulse that's running hard.
The strings are bowed to tremble
And the amps begin to retard.
The music slows after a climax.
The piano hammers out the chords.
It winds down to the finish
Like an echo from the sound boards.

01/12/2012

Figure it out

I can't figure it out. / Is it your bright blue eyes, / that wonderful winning smile, / or that figure that other women would kill for / That makes my mind, / Both waking and sleeping, / dwell on only you…/ until I find myself wasting away my day? / And I often wonder / If I could measure up / to my own quiet fantasies / for surely I could fall and crush my own ego. / Could I take the shock / to my soul and heart / to be dumped by you / like I've been dumped before in matters of the heart? / Is not the heart itself / meant to be proffered / on the alter of love / to be used or abused at the whim of a lover? / Maybe a heart is soft / because it is tenderized / and beaten like a flank steak / with a wooden mallet and bruised beyond belief.

06-27-2002

FINAL SALUTE

I saw a friend off to the eternities today
His leaving me seemed to be very untimely
And with grief in my heart I saw him on his way
Knowing that we, left behind, must follow eventually

Carrying the casket I was aware of the weight,
Not that of the empty Temple of my friend,
But of hearts near breaking in sorrow great
At the absence of his spirit with his fellow men.

Many of his friends line the walk this day
As we pass slowly towards the gray hearse
That will carry him, but not his memory, away
To be lowered gently into the dark earth.

As a final salute we stand at the grove
And place our flowers upon his last repose
Before he comes forth with the brave
By the promise of our savior made long ago

(written upon the death of Larry Mandell,
Reserve Washoe County Deputy)

First time

It must have been the first time,
    But it was so long ago. It seems
Like I was always meant to rhyme
    To find that word to shape a dream.
I see pictures made of flowery words
    That paint with brushes in your mind
That forms an image at times obscure
    If that's the way your tastes inclined.
Picking words out one by precious one
    To draw the reader through my eyes
To see the moment that it's taken from
    The lay of the land, how it lies.
Or picture a person – a shape of face
    A curve of the body that I describe,
The shade of the skin that hints of race
    The ripple of muscle, an eye that cried.
The flow of a river, a rush of wind
    The sound of the traffic rushing past
The birds singing spring from yonder limb
    The whine of a puppy, a rustle of grass.
When first you use words, I explain,
    Your mind paints its picture, black and white,
Right here on the paper, flat and plain
    Shaded and colored till you get it right.

04/06/2012

FLAMES OF SUMMER

That hot summer wind
Again scorches my lawn.
The mountains are dry,
Snow's missing this year.
The heat starts building
Every morning past dawn
Till the temperature rises
Until it can sear.

Tomorrow, in the evening,
Thunder clouds will appear
And bring the promise
Of thunder and rain.
But with the thunder
Lightning too will appear
And bring summer fires
Across mountain and plain.

And it happens again
In this parched land
The fires of drought
Light the evening sky
And the heavy smoke
Lifts from the brand
That marks this land
Like a steers thigh.

This great western desert
Shows many a sign
That chisels of flame
Have carved the landscape
By burning the brush
In long spotting lines

That spread and curve
        Like a wafted cape.

The smoke always rises
        After a summer rain
Sometimes it just smolders
        But it often flares
Stripping the dry land
        Of springs dry remain
Sprung from spring showers
        As often it dares.

And we run out
        With sirens and lights
To save our homes
        From tongues of flame
That lap their way,
        An awful fearful sight
Toward our little towns
        As if by aim.

And usually we win,
        But occasionally, we lose
And we get away
        To plant fields again
And we build our houses
        Just wherever we choose
Across scars of ashes
        Covered with grass again.

We ignore natures warning
        That we've seen before
It's only a folktale
        Some passed down lore
That tells of fires

Which had steadfastly bore
Down on this city
In times called yore.

But trees have recovered
And flowers grow back
As sure as winter
spreads its water about
'Cause old mother nature
Doesn't color in black.
Streams flow into rivers
And nurture the trout.

But flames of summer
Will some day return
As certain as seasons
Will come every year
They're fueled by grasses
Which really do burn
And men who firefight
Will use their gear.

Perhaps they'll save us,
They'll earn their pay
'Cause we build house
Where flames often play.
Perhaps we will learn
Before we get gray
Build houses in cities
Not in fires way.

07/02/2001

FLEETING SUNLIGHT

There is nothing quite as fleeting
As those fading rays of sunlight
When the sun behind the mountains
Paint the clouds with colors bright.
Orange, gold, and silver shine
To finish off a cloudy day
And those colors quickly dimming
Seem to cool to black and gray.
Drawn as moths to the brilliant sunsets
Are the hearts and eyes of poets
As they set the words to paper
As they feel it and they note it
And it stirs within them Muses
Who bring forth the rhymes and rhythm
And form the verse and stanzas
To reflect that moment of time.
Can you fail but to record it
And paint it for your reader,
The colors and the feelings
Put to tempo and to meter.
Grab your stylist and your tablet
Or your clipboard and your pen
And make the moment last forever
As it is and as it's been.

12-16-2012

FLOAT

Ah! to float in the water is so fine
To relieve all the pains and relax
To stretch and flex the muscles all over
To get a nice tan on our backs.

The sun and the water have combined
To form our own world away from home
To find ourselves anew for each other
To really live in this world of our own.

No rules to hold back our feelings.
No reason for anything but our harmony
No people to make us too self-conscious
But each other to make our own company.

Together to find what life is about,
To explore without bonds, without fear,
To look at the world in its pureness,
And yes, the comfort of having you near.

Our own world is built in dreams.
It is ours only to share and love.
To commune with the island of hope
Created in our minds by our love.

Sharing moments like this is what life's about.
It's what people like us were made for.
It's what the world needs for its problems.
It's the part of life I adore.

Help me build on this dream of life
Founded on thoughts of love and good.
A better world it would form, if only
Each person this dream understood.

1970

FOG

A vale of fog rises from the field
Covering the moon and shading out the stars
Casting its form in the valley as a blanket
Curling and dancing in the light of cars.

Fog is so thin, so easy to move aside
But it closes behind as if nothing passed
Leaving no sign of the passers trail.
No trail in fog will ever last.

This is also true in the lives of men.
It's called the path of least resistance.
Yet, as fog, it covers all signs
That the traveler has to show his existence.

By overcoming resistance we cut a path
Which can never be filled again
And by the cutting of a straight path
We as boys will mature into men.

So don't cut the easy way through fog.
Cut a path that shows others the way.
That both of you and others can follow
For that , unlike fog, will always stay.

1970

Life goes on

FOR CARSON SMITH
against his wishes but in his memory

Life goes on... at least for some
Or at least for the most
But our group is missing one
Who at times had been our host.

But that beating force is still
That once pumped sure and strong.
Quiet now, his heart, his mill,
That should have served him long.

His ceaseless banter now has ceased.
His stories at last all told.
He never left a room in peace
Or let his chair get cold

His opinion always found a voice
And he shared it more than once.
To listen could be luck or choice
And he wouldn't pull the punch.

And he'll be missed, that Carson guy
We'll remember him so long.
I'll just read this and pause and sigh
And wonder why he's gone.

03/06/03

For Jan's Dog

Our furry legged friends
With their wagging tails
Give us such love
That other loves pale.
And when one passes
To her just reward
The loss to us
Is especially hard.

But of our dogs
It is often said
Go directly to Heaven
Plump and well fed.
They're groomed by angels
Until their masters pass
When they are united
In heaven at last.

Tears we shed now,
We feel such loss.
We miss our puppies
We may feel cross.
But remember the love
That they always gave
The sloppy wet kisses
And tails that wave.

And remember their moments
When giving us care,
They were our bosses
All covered with hair.
But now they're gone
But not far away
It won't be long
Till together we play.

I know it's sad
And hearts can hurt
But it's her shell
That's under the dirt.
She's up there playing
And having such fun
And waiting for mommy
When her time's done.

05/03/2004

FREE AGENT

Forces are changing my life which I cannot control
      Gripping my life and shoving it in different ways
Changing those patterns which have been already formed
      What can I do? Where can I seek council?
How can I guide the remainder of my days
      That my life and destiny may not be harmed
I know not, But there must be open ways.
      I must be a free agent unto myself.
I must have choice of my life and will.
      I cannot be stuck on the back shelf.
This can't ever wholly, justifiably reconcile.
      Therefore I must try with all my might
To control those things which control my soul
      And set my life and ways just right
So I in the end reach my goal.

1972

FROGS THAT CROAK

Frogs that croak
    Fires that smoke
Mornings so chilly
    You need a coat.
Streams running by,
    The Mosquito, The fly,
Rattling cars leave
    Dust in your eye.
Girls that talk,
    Five mile walk,
Boots too tight,
    Holes in your sock.
Tenting at night,
    Stars out bright,
The heavens so close,
    Touch them, You might.
Birds in the trees,
    Needles and leaves.
To chop up wood
    Roll up your sleeves.

6-13-86

Four Paws

Four little paws are rarely at rest
        As she scurries all over the place.
That little pug girl all shiny and black
        And her nose is pushed flat on her face.
She snuggles and burrows just to keep warm
        Under blankets and laundry so soft.
They're hot from the dryer, sparkling clean.
        A pug's nest of now wrinkled cloth.
If you're cooking bacon she's at your feet
        As soon as it gets to the pan,
She scratches, she whimpers, and dances around
        To get a rasher from her favorite man.
She'd settle for half a pizza
        Or pieces of your burger and fries
Or hunks of warm bread off your hoagie.
        It won't ever show on her thighs
She's a whole lot of love for the money.
        She'll take you along for a walk.
She'll even pretend that she listens
        When it's quiet and you just need to talk.
12-18-11

GOD'S DEEDS

Sometimes things just don't go right
      And sometimes you are blue.
At times like these, Just look around
      And see what God had done for you.

He made all the worlds and the stars
      That are spread through the universe
And made the smallest tiny thing
      And the mighty roaring surf.

God has done all these things for us
      And even sacrificed His Son,
That He may show us all new life
      If we but come to Him come.

So don't be sad or weary grow
      For all your trials of life.
Think of all that God has done
      To make our lives just right.

1970

GODS' CANVAS

Do you look to that moment
                    That moment each day
When the sunshine is fading
                    And will soon go away.
When the colors of evening
                    Are drawn to the sky
With the orange and gold
                    That tickle the eye.
The clouds light up each evening
                    And put on a show
That shames all the artists
                    Whose paintings can't glow.
And the sight touches deep
                    And stirs you way down
For the fire's in the sky
                    And not in the town.
And the cool of the evening
                    Blows down from the hill
And the frogs and the crickets
                    Can hardly keep still
But break into their songs
                    That will draw a new mate
'Cause we all want to snuggle
                    As the evening draws late.
And the cold winds of winter
                    Will come soon enough
And make watching of sunsets
                    Just for the tough.
But in evenings you'll see me
                    With eyes on the sky
For I call God an Artist
                    With His canvas up High.

08/19/2001

GOING BACK

You can't go back.

I've heard that before but I always come back.

I was born here in this valley. I was raised here and I always come back.

I can still go back to my old neighborhood or I can just close my eyes and name all the people on the block. I remember their children and where some of them worked. I even know where some of them work now

We knew each other back then. We knew each others habits and problems. We knew who was drunk and who was sober. We knew who was sick and who was well. The widows got their walks shoveled after a storm because it was the right thing to do. Old Mrs. Palmer called me the sidewalk fairy.

The alley was a main thoroughfare for us kids. We knew all the back yards and all the short cuts through the two empty lots.

Sometimes I drive through the neighborhood just to mind trip. Most the houses are still there. But just below the area has gone commercial. I drive down the alley and I remember the people and the kids.

I miss my tree house. After dad died the lot was subdivided and they took the tree down to put up an apartment. One of the guys at the jail tells all the other inmates about that tree house. It was a platform we built in the fruit tree. We put a wooden ladder from the platform to the top of the tree and tied it really good. Over the years the ladder grew into the tree. It was so solid you could climb up and sit on the top step and look out over the whole neighborhood, Out over the fields to the west, Out to the tracks to the north. I can still close my eyes and see the sights from the ladder clearly in my mind.

The hill down the street to the east was the greatest entertainment for us kids. Biking, skateboarding, or sledding depending on the season. I couldn't tell you how many times I got going too fast on that hill and crashed and burned on that asphalt. Sparks was a small town then. We knew everybody for three blocks around our house and Reno was that town over there. We were miles apart. Going to Reno was a special occasion because we kept to our town.

Keitzke Lane and Plumb Lane were dirt roads and not all the roads in Sparks were paved yet either.

A kid could wander the streets alone and talk to everyone. There were no strangers in Sparks. Everyone knew you and your folks. We went to church together we went to each others churches just to be with your friends.
You shopped at your friend's store because he was your friend. Not because they were having a sale. You were loyal. You supported them and they supported you. That way you all ate.
At the end of the street was the stockyards. We would listen to the auctioneer babble.
"Will you give me fifty?"
"Fifty, will you give me fifty five?"
"Fifty five, Will you give me Sixty?"
All we did was collect the bottles from under the seats. They knew we were down there. We would take those bottles to the mom and pop store across the street and cash them in. a few cents apiece added up when candy bars were a dime and a pop was fifteen cents. We thought we were kings.
I haven't thought of that for years. We'd spend hot summer mornings on the wooden fences looking over the livestock. It never occurred to us that all those sheep and steers would grace or tables next week, All those ribs on the hoof.
I'm lucky I can drive across town and be in the old neighborhood. But really all I have to do is close my eyes and I'm back there in both space and time when the houses might have been a different color and I was still young.
Ah, Yes, the house, the neighborhood, and the memories.
01-11-2000

GOODBYE SAM

Sometimes, old friend, you get what you've prayed for
And you slipped away from us alone in the night
But that is the way you wanted to go....
When it was your time, and without a fight.

We all said goodbye to you in different ways.
I talked to you alone with your casket open
Before the others arrived for your little service.
So cold, So pale, So thin. Your presence but token.

But I felt you there, So I said goodbye
As I had done each week at your home
As I visited with and checked on you
Because you were both old and alone.

They say you go to your reward, to what you've earned
But I think you've rested enough the last days of your life.
Now you will celebrate with friends "Who've gone before"
Those missing from your family, your brother and your wife.

You may squeeze again your accordion, not some stupid little harp
Because it seemed at the last that it weighed more than you.
And you won't be slowed by your walker or canes.
Those old legs will be working like new.

I pray that you've gone to a better place
Though the other option was more than a threat.
You're better off now than lying in bed.
May God's Mercy far outweigh your debt.

12/3/2001

GUILD OF THE GUN

I don't want to write a poem for you
and I don't want one written for me.

I just want to watch my children grow up
and live to the age of a tree

I want to remember the time that we shared
and watch each other retire.

And shake our heads and our hair that's gray
when we see the new guys they hire.

I want to hear the stories you tell,
though I've heard them again and again.

The tails of the busts, the chases, and the trials
How we shipped them all off to the pen.

I want to see your face in wrinkles
Carved deep with the passage of time,

With a crick in your back and a wink in your eye,
Aged and mellowed like wine.

I want us still friends as the decades go by,
Hand in hand we'll grow old.

For we're cast together in the Guild of the Gun
And God Himself broke the mold.

So go on my friend, Be noble and brave,
And leave your mark on the wall.

They'll remember us and the deeds we have done
And the way we've answered the Call.

11-22-96

HALCYON SPRING

The sound of the water in the pond
Bubbling out of the fountain so clear
Soothing the noise of the puppies at play
And the birds at the feeder I hear.

The smell of the fresh watered lawn
And the colors of fruit trees in bloom.
The greens in the garden are starting to spread.
They'll add to our salads quite soon

The swings, now empty, shift in the breeze
Waiting for our grandkids to play
'cause that's why we put them there.
They'll be here later today.

But it's quiet here and we can enjoy the spring
With the halcyon sounds and the smells
Of the warming earth and the running water
And the flowers displaying their petals.

4/27/2009

HANKS

A blue candle flickers in the night.
        The flame licks the air as it burns
To remind us of one who burned bright
        But is now passed where none returns.
He was once on of a special few
        In whom we trusted to serve and care.
One that wore a star and we knew
        If we needed him he was there.
But we turn now … and he's gone,
        There is not but emptiness, but memory,
A hollow is left, something went wrong,
        And now we weep – missing him sorely.
I know it is, "the way of all flesh"
        But somehow it doesn't seem fair
That one so young, so strong, so fresh,
        Has joined the legions that are "Over There".
In the Great Beyond he waits for us
        And we wear black bands for him.
We stand in ranks, somber and hushed
        And the pipes shall rend the wind.
May their tune carry to him our loss.
        May he know in heaven we shall miss
His company, his smile, his voice. We pause
        To remember HANKS leaving us behind like this.

09/28/2013

The Harbingers of Winter

The wind swirls the leaves down the street.
      Yellows and reds flashing their colors
Against the black of the paving.
      The colors of fall as we motor.

The greens are fading as days pass
      Into the cool winds of fall.
And mornings show frost clinging
      To the roofs and the shaded wall.

Joggers in their hats and sweats
      Run on the crumbling shoulder
Where they ran in T's and shorts
      Before the year got older.

Soon the pumpkins will become lanterns
      Or filling for some pies
And the children trick for candy,
      See the sparkle in their eyes.

And we dream of ham and turkey
      Roasted with a glaze
And fields of drying seed corn
      Shaped into a maze.

The harbingers of winter
      Make blue skies fade to gray.
And the birds reluctantly fly southerly
      And they won't be back till May.

10/20/2002

THE HOMOPTEROUS THEORY

There are as many theories of leadership as there are schools of leadership in the world. They range from the Charismatic Theory to the Hereditaric Theory and any combination of these theories that can be imagined.

I would like to present a theory not usually considered when enumerating ways to progress up the leadership ladder on the way to the top. This theory would be titled the Homopterous Theory of Leadership. I would postulate that this particular method would define many organizations current method of selecting the promising leadership candidates and separating them from the run of the mill rank and file members of any organization.

This theory receives its descriptive name from the world of nature. The Order of Homopterous of the Class Insecta are, by definition, Insects. Further defined in this smaller Order Homopterous which includes the Family Diaspididae. Further subdividing to contain the Genus of Aphia (aphids), and the Genus Cicadidae (cicada).

What uniquely defines these two Genus of insects describes succinctly the actions of the aspiring leadership candidate I wish to define in this theory. As defined in the Second College Edition of the Webster's New World Dictionary page 672 and continuing onto page 673 Homopterous is defined as "Belonging to an Order (Homoptera) of insects with sucking mouth parts... as aphids, cicada, scale insects, etc."

I see the relationship to the human race easy to explain as the very next two entries in the dictionary are Homosapiens and Homosexual respectively. I postulate that this is not coincidental but truly a sign to any free minded individual that climbing up the ladder of success in this manner casts doubt on your human sexual orientation.

Surely when you look at your particular organization you see members of the upper staff that have no obvious qualification other than being effective under the desk and manipulating the zipper of an even higher member of said staffing system. These members are proof positive of the Peter Principle that has been often expounded in modern circles and I find reference may be to an actual Peter (or if you insist Male Member or Phallus) which may also be more than a Freudian slip in this context. Surely by examining this above postulation the obvious conclusion would be that numerous administrative staff members that appear to have no meaningful or obvious useful skills may have provided other services in relieving the stresses and pent up emotions or fluids of a senior management officer.

The Homopterous Theory would by this reason be validated and should be included in instruction to those who would prosper by climbing up the zipper of success.

Submitted
Kevin D. Lieby,
Student of Human Behavior dated 02/06/2002

I Fly My Flag

My neighbor scrapes the frost from his windshield
      As I raise a flag on the front of my house.
I never considered myself overly patriotic
      But I have defended the land in which I've grown.
I did what I was asked to do
      And I am not ashamed to be called a veteran.
Though the war I was in was not popular
      It had to be done, and by me, not by "someone".
If something is worth something it is to be earned.
      Sometimes the pay is in sweat, Sometimes in blood.
Sometimes our scars show red, other scars hide in our heart,
      But we've spent our time in the sand or the mud.
That red stripe on the flag is my blood.
      That Blue is the sky over my town.
That star is the state in which I live
      And I pity the coward that would try to take it down.
I still cry when I hear people sing our anthem
      As the wind stirs and makes my flag wave.
I cry not in fear, But with tears of pride
      Because My Land is free and I am not a slave.
If you are not ready to die for that flag
      You are not worthy to raise it as your ensign.
That is my flag. That I have chosen to fly
      And I have given my time to make it mine.

11-04-2001

I HEAR YOUR PAIN

I hear your pain
        You whine like a bad brake job.
You say you're beat.
        The man had his way with you
With his black stick.
        He's laid about your ribs and back.
I hear your pain
        But I witness not the black and blue.
I've carried that stick
        And applied it a time or two.
But it was there
        As a tool close at hand
Because you showed me
        By your acts, not just your words
That you did not respect
        The laws of this great land.
You can walk here
        Both day and night
Because I walk here
        Between you and the dangerous dark.
I wear the armor
        And I bear the scars myself
That you have the freedom
        To read poetry in the park.
And I read also
        Raising my voice in this verse.
I too have poems
        And also have the right to read
The words I've written
        But I don't whine and curse
Because I have poems

To fill my brothers need.
I write my badge.
My pen has a black barrel
As does my gun
And I find I can use each,
And use them well,
On those of those who have gone feral
And prey on others
Just because they come within reach.
I can come here
And read a poem of my work.
I do not fear
What lies waiting out in the dark
Nor what it is
It plans to hit or hurt
For I am ready
With both my gun and heart.
You can read poems.
You can say anything you want
Because I am here
To uphold that Bill of Rights
That frees the words
Though some but raze and taunt
The work I perform.
For I fought the fights
And I have lain
In the damp sands of a jungle
Just for your right
To read poems in the night
To say I'm wrong
To use a stick to strike and pummel
On your tender back
Then listen to you gripe.

If you read them
        On that infamous square in China
You would be goo
        Dripping off their iron tracks
To read no more
        About phallus or vagina
As you read here
        With your mocha or your coffee blacks.
Maybe I shouldn't read
        The precious words of my pen
For you haven't paid,
        Like I have, with time and blood.
You haven't seen death
        A hundred times in a hundred ways
As I have seen
        In the streets and in the mud.
You have not learned
        The lessons found in war.
You have not felt
        Lead rip holes in your tender flesh
Nor watched the doctor
        Cut down into your own gut
To remove the slug
        From where it came to rest.
But this I've done
        That we could read our poems
Here in the park.
        Not hiding in some quiet alley
Like some must do
        Because where they have their homes
They do not have
        The rights my presence guarantees.

05/05/2001

I MISS

I miss when you're away at camp…
I miss waking up, rolling over and saying, "Good morning beautiful."
Then seeing your smile that brightens the day as the morning sun.
I miss kissing you and the pack goodbye before running off to work
As you sit in bed sharing with them your breakfast of chocolate covered cookies
And the chocolate makes your kisses even sweeter than ever.
I miss calling you from work just to touch base,
And enjoying the pleasant sound of your voice
That has the power to change my mood
And make my day pass so much better.
I miss coming home and shouting, "Honey I'm home."
And being greeted by you and not just a pack
Of lonely dogs licking and barking their greetings.
I miss sitting with you at the dinner table,
(Sorry but Gramps' company just doesn't do it)
Watching you feed the dogs the scraps from your plate
After you're done as they eat carefully from your fork.
I miss you typing away on your laptop in bed,
While I read quietly next to you till it's time to sleep.
I miss snuggling up next to you as we go to sleep.
I find comfort in your arms knowing you're there
By my side, sharing warmth, sharing time,
Sharing the very air we breathe this moment.
I guess I just miss you, every minute you're gone
From my side I feel all empty and hollow
Like a chocolate Easter egg.

06/30/2005

I SHRINK

Why do I back away?
Why do I shrink at your touch?
Women! Look at my heart.
See the scars that you've left.

I used to love love.
I used to love too much,
Giving right from the start,
Always in the end bereft.

I am beginning to think
That love is a broken crutch
That leaves but pain and smart
And cuts with slashes so deft

That I cannot again love.
I cannot give again such
As I did before impart,
For there is so little left.

Mark this, You ladies fair,
When I wince at your touch,
I flee from Cupids dart
Lest my heart again be cleft.

08/13/2001

Iwant to say---I'm done

I want to wake up in the morning
With the sun shining into my bedroom window.
I want to eat my breakfast in leisure
Not throwing it down straight from the box.
I want to listen to quiet Jazz
Not the morning traffic report.
I want to drive into town midmorning
Not rushing headlong during rush hour
With the other time crazed demons
Being propelled by the clock and horsepower.
I don't want to search franticly
For that all elusive parking space,
Then hurry along the sidewalk
To reach the office and punch that clock.
To spend the day glancing
At that slowly moving clock
Until it says you can finally
Race the traffic back home.
I want to sit in the park,
By the river, and listen to the water
Rushing like the morning traffic
Past my unmoving park bench.
I want to listen to the ducks
Paddling in the slow pools
As they tell each other
Of the pending handouts of bread.
I want to scribble away happily

On the notebooks from my bag
Telling you I finally have time
To write what I want to write.
To pen verse after verse
Uninterrupted by illiterate supervisors
Who couldn't understand the words
I choose to fill my paper.
I want a modicum of peace
After decades of serving myself
Up to the pressure of work
For those dollars that pays homage
To the hungry mouths of cash boxes
Open like the beaks of chicks
Awaiting the worms and insects
From their mother's overworked bill.
I am soon done with this labor
And I wait for the gold watch to come ---
As if that makes up for the years
Of tacit slavery to that paycheck.

03-07-2005

I woke up this morning

I woke up this morning
And the winds of storm were blowing
But the bed was warm
And the thermostat said sixty-eight.

But today is Saturday
But everyday is a Saturday
Since I have retired
And I can now sleep late.

I wake up each day
Instead of running off to work.
And I can snuggle in
With my beautiful bride

I still have dreams
About the old working life.
I hear they fade away
Slowly ebbing as the tide.

I still have friends
From the old sweat shop
That I call on occasion
When I find an excuse.

We share many times
And we plan going out
'cause we now have time
And we're now on the loose.

I send them an e-mail
And they'll read it someday
If they ever log in.
So I remind their answering machine.

Now I'll play Solitaire
Since the computer is up
And I have all this time
And it's to cold to go fishing.

11-27-07

IF YOU WERE MINE

04/27/96

If you were mine
I would write sonnets,
Shakespeare and Chaucer
Would envy the form.
The meter and rhyme
Would be so sublime
That my work would
Be far above norm.
If you were mine
I could write stories
Michener and Clavell would
Throw out their pens,
They could not compete
With the inspired elite,
They'd give up and
Go party with friends.
Then I could spend
All day just writing,
Making love come out
Line penned upon line,
Inspired by every movement
You make passing by
I would write volumes...
If you were mine.

Alas! I am lonely!
My pen not inspired.
I stare at the
Paper, clean and white.
The words cannot flow
When Love doesn't know
That the poet's alone
This warm night.
His heart feels the
Call of the Muses
As he labors to
Write what he feels.
It brings sharpened pain
To see you again
In his mind, for
His love he conceals.
He suffers in silence
Alone with the stars.
He dreams of tomorrows
That will never transpire.
For she doesn't care
That he's always there.
He's but a poet
What could he desire.

JJ

Old JJ Straits sure liked to kick ass
In this county, not long ago
He never took shit
From the Sun Valley scum
And he told them all
Just where to go.
He never backed down
But was often backed up
He was so good at stirring the shit.
This portly old cherub
Could sure dish it out.
His ways were 'as good as they get'.
He went the full thirty
Sometimes ducking IA's
Those years were so full of events.
If you looked at his unit
Most of the time
More than his record had dents.
If you were a 'runnin'
He'd breathe down your neck
Till he rode you right into the ground
If you were a hiding
You just couldn't move
He was there if you just looked around.
There's many a scumbag
That's cooling his heals
With mail marked just "N.S.P."
'cause they couldn't outrun
JJ and his gun
And he put them just where they should be.
But thirty's the limit
The fun's got to stop
He's getting "too old" for the work.
Only a fool would
Say that to his face
'Cause he'd reach up and give you a jerk.
But Jerry it's time.
Put that damn gun away.
Turn your uniforms in to supply.
Your poor old lady's
Got chores to be done.
You'll never escape, just you try.

06-26-2001

JUST A FEELING

10-23-2000

You always remember those times in your life when you feel the hair on the back of your neck stand up. The times when your senses stretch beyond what you can perceive and it tells you what you couldn't know.

We've all had those moments. Maybe we feel someone's looking at us behind our backs. Maybe we know something is lurking around the bend in the road. And we hesitate before we look. We're sure he has just turned away or else we just gave it enough time to get off the road.

We had a hunch or just a feeling of something about to happen. Yet we didn't know why or how or when. We just knew.

Could we voice it?

Could we articulate our premonitions?

Could we explain our fears?

I've had to. I've had to in court. I've had to explain why I was aware that a man was where he couldn't be known to be. And why I'm alive, and he isn't.

I remember the night before when in Briefing we got an ATL on a man wanted for crimes in about seventeen states, from Tennessee to Nevada. We copied down the description of both him and his vehicle, possible weapons, place last seen, direction of travel, and his criminal profile or M.O.

It had been a quiet and uneventful night. Washoe Valley had been a boring community on graveyard shift. It was time I was heading north to gas up and punch out. I was never in a hurry to get back. A slow and observant return meant you worked your way in.

I had come over Washoe Hill past the Jubilee Club. The lighting sky shed dim outlines to the cottonwoods but not yet enough to see any detail.

I had just passed Laramie when I saw the car. It was parked on the opposite side of the highway pointed southbound. No lights showed from it and it looked abandoned.

There was no traffic. I went down a quarter mile and hooked a U-turn. I got close enough To see the plates. They were from Tennessee. This was Lynch's car. It looked like he had abandoned it on U.S. 395.

Before I got closer I scanned the approach and the fields on both sides. I didn't want to be jumped if he was out there somewhere. I saw nothing but the backs of houses and their yards. Nothing was moving except some horses and they didn't act disturbed.

I keyed my radio and advised dispatch I was 10-6 on a 10-37 at 395 and Laramie. I described the vehicle and read off the plates. I could almost hear a half dozen tired deputies snapping full awake. Then I heard the alert tones call out "V-victor, 10-99, F-frank, consider armed and dangerous." I knew units fifteen miles away were lighting up and shattering the night with their sirens. The closest called "In route from Sun Valley Code Three, ETA fifteen." Other unit called in indicating their routes.

I slid out of my car. I had a quarter of an hour before the sky would be colored by the lights of all those units.

I got low behind the door of my unit and pulled out my Smith and Wesson.

I did a crouch walk out of my headlights toward the car. As I got close that proverbial hair raised up on the back of my neck. Yet I had no indication Lynch was still around. I went into survival mode.

My spotlights in the back window of his car showed no movement. If he looked back all he would see would be the lights of my headlights and spotlights shining his way. A wall of light and glare. He couldn't see me or my movements.

I neared the bumper on the left side of his car squatting way down below the trunkline. I was below his line of sight.

I reached forward and touched the trunk lid. I froze a minute just to feel if there was any movement in the car. I pushed down on the trunk lid with my left hand to make sure it was locked down or lock it down if it wasn't. My right hand held the gun ready to shoot through the trunk if it moved. It was locked.

I moved out left into the travel lane of 395.

I moved out a few feet and edged up the side of the car crouching low and weapon on the ready towards the back seat of the car. I did a pop up, peek and drop. the first peek just to see if a second was safe. I saw nothing in the rear seat area that threatened me.

I inched forward up and took a longer peek. Seeing nothing again I eased to the back edge of the drivers door. Every sense was locked on that area, I popped up to peek in the drivers seat area.

Shit. There he was with one of those eighteen inch screwdrivers in his right hand. If I hadn't been back and locked on him with my gun I'd have been skewered.

"Freeze you son of a bitch!" I yelled, "Get your hands up where I can see them!"

His hands came up slowly. They came into the light empty. I knew the screwdriver was still somewhere inside. I reached forward and flipped the door open and backed into the street. "You move - you're dead!" I assured him. And he shouted back "OK, You got me. OK"

With my gun pointed dead center of his reclined body I backed away a few more feet into the roadway and took a couple of deep breaths. I let my heart beat slow. It was beating so loud I could hear it plainly.

I didn't have many options. The occasional car was going by in the growing light and traffic would only get worse. I instructed him to keep his hands in the light and wiggle slowly out the now open door. He understood if the hands disappeared I would kill him.

He scooted out toward me and eased out of the car. I commanded him to kneel in the roadway. I observed his beltline for weapons and didn't see any. I moved to my right, towards my car. I had him lean forward and go to a prone position. I ordered him to put his arms spread-eagle and spread his legs. He was told to turn his head to the right so he could not see me or my movements.

He didn't seem too surprised in a minute when my knee dropped into the middle of his back and I had him bring his hand back for cuffing. This is not easy left handed with the gun pointed at his head.

I holstered my weapon now and patted him for weapons. I took a moment to look back and see the screwdriver on the floor mat. I then returned to my car and told the responding units I had him in custody.

He yelled at me. "Don't leave me in the middle of the fucking highway!"

I opened the back door of my unit and closed the front door. I went to him and eased him up holding his shoulder and arm locked solid so he could not turn on me.

I guided him towards the rear seat of the car and got him in without a struggle. I secured his seatbelt and slammed the door. I could breathe again. I pulled out my clipboard and began making notes. I could hear the sirens far away in the distance. They would be here in a minute because sound does not travel far in this narrow valley.

Hell, there was a line of red and blue lights coming toward me at ninety mile an hour, bumper to bumper. Then there was the brakes locking and the cars forming in a formation around the scene. I waited calmly in front of my unit.

"Where is he?"
"Did you get him?"
"Yes, he's hooked and in the cage."
"You didn't wait for us?"
"You were a long way off and I ran out of time."

I let them tow the car and I took my prisoner to jail. He passed out on the way and I thought he was drunk. He did smell of alcohol. I half dragged him into the booking office. Then he just died.

The man who had laid in wait for me to kill me just minutes before had died of a heart attack.

I later learned that he had been released from Tennessee State Prison because his heart had gone bad on him. I think he wanted to go out in style. So he did his one man crime spree across the U.S. But it and his heart stopped in Reno.

JUST A HUMBLE POET

I am just a poet
      That means I'm better than you.
And I am published
      And my writing's important too.
You are nothing
      If you can't write like me
Or have other talents
      That could lend you credibility.

I'm not a snob
      I'm an artist of some note.
Ask me anything
      And I will brag or I will gloat
But who are you?
      I doubt if you can even read
Or listen intently
      As my ego fills its need.

I love writing
      My words will last forever.
They're carved in brass
      Because my topics are so clear.
So stand back people,
      I know you can hardly wait
To shake the hand
      Of someone really great.

09-10-2001

JUST A RIDE.

08-07-00

I know it's just a ride. I know my kids have ridden it already today. But can I face it? Can I face Paramount's Demon, that steel roller coaster?

The Grizzly was exciting and more my style. Built of wood like all the roller coasters I have faced so far. They simply go up and then race down. They go around a few corners, up and down a few times and you're done.

I've watched my fifteen, thirteen and eleven-year-olds screaming with joy as they race with hands upreached around this course. And now they've shamed me, their own father, to take these fateful steps to the gate of "The Demon".

We wait in line and I stare at the cold steel of the cars and track that will soon spread the contents of my stomach and maybe portions of my bloody carcass across the fertile real-estate of San Jose. Cold steel, like the blades of a million swords that have hacked the tender flesh of men through the ages. Cold steel, not the warm wood of the forest and home, holds my fate.

The cars rattle to a stop. The laughing riders jump out of the cars with the exuberance of youth and the lilt of confidence. Yet I face my fears, I tell my son in law that I'd rather face a man with a gun than this ride. I know what it's like to stop a pellet of lead with my flesh. I've watched a skilled surgeon cut into my abdomen and pull out a scrap of metal.

But this ride goes up. I've told my kids with an earnest voice that I fear heights. I would do almost anything to avoid them. But, I can't act a coward in front of my children.

I crawl down into the car. My mind can't help thinking it's the size of a casket. The padded restraints pull down over my shoulders. I knew they needed padded steel to keep anymore innocent people from following others into the abyss of death. It clicks as it ratchets into place and I find heavy steal grips welded onto the outside. I grasp them with the strength that has sent hardened criminals to their knees.

My children, two ahead of me and one at my side, talk excitedly as I face my doom.

The car jerks forward, pulling us to the chain that drags us away from the earth into the warm California sky. I sweat. Isn't it supposed to get cooler at such heights.

I, with false bravado shout, "Arg, We're all going to die." as we come to the top of the steel chain and slowly go over the summit. I'm sure the bones in my hands are snapping as my grip tightens into what, I'm sure, is pre-Rigor Mortis and we fall into the zero gravity that in my terror will loosen only in the hands of a coroner.

Quickly we reach the bottom and are wrenched into the first barrel roll. I feel the coke of an hour ago heave in my stomach trying to find its way to freedom. Then it's over the top dropping, dropping into another barrel roll. I re-swallow my coke and wait for the blackness of oblivion to stop my heart.

We bank left and up then left again into, oh no, not now, a double corkscrew to the right. I yell again, "We're all going to die." And I'm crushed into my seat by the inertia of the speeding car. Surely we will be flung to our end through that fence. Yes, Just like a cheese grater. Minced into the afterlife to be gathered by one of my fellow officers and thrown, piece by piece, into one of those heavy plastic bags I carry in the back of my patrol car. I'm going to be maggot meat. This Demon is carrying carrion. I want to die at work like a real man. Not squashed like a bug on a windshield. Hold together demon car, Hold together.

Suddenly we begin to slow and turn toward the safety of the loading platform. Fate has smiled on me one time and I've made the end.

There's no one waiting to get on at the platform and my kids shout with glee, "Let's go again, Daddy, Let's go again.'

The ride attendants ask if everyone is ready again and my heart sinks.

"Once more unto the breach, dear friends, once more." Shakespeare, Henry the V, Act III. Scene 1.

The End

JUST IMAGINE

Why need we dream of purple trees
     When Lilacs grace yet our yards
Or dream of pink trees bursting forth
     When cherried trees bloom hard?

Oh, we need not look for colors bright
     Or plants that may look strange
Search here on earth, Just left and right
     At what springtime will arrange.

Paintbrushes look dipped in colors true
     In shades from yellow through orange to red
Yet phlox are wild from white to purple
     Spread low, to make a flower bed.

Our tulips blossom from the mud
     And splash green leaves with color.
And iris tall and delicate of bud
     Graced the gardens of my mother.

The popcorn tree show balls of white
     That looks the world like the snow
That's on the ground just underneath
     Through which the tulips show.

That cactus reaches from the rocks
For it doesn't need much water.
Its skin is wax and armed with barbs
As if sculptured by a potter

The smooth white bark adorns the beech
Yet the big trees sport barks of red
And the woods that color right on through,
So's the cedar, it is said.

Are apples red? unless they're green
But of course they could be yellow
And range in taste from sweet to sharp
Or a taste that's bright or mellow.

Are bluebirds blue? And cardinals red?
Does yellow look good on tweedy?
Do toucans look agog in colors
As if painted by a committee?

Just look around, It's springtime you fool!
The land bursts forth in color.
You need not dream in black and white.
Look outside. It's almost summer!

04-09-2001

LATE GOOD-BYES

You never get to say goodbye
 to those you really cherish.
At least that has been true
 in my case, when they perish.
        You see them, then they're gone
              Suddenly before you know it
        They're snatched away from life
              And you're left to face it.
You go on fighting a good fight
 But wishing you could tell
Your old friend what they really
 meant before their final bell.
        What would you have said if you
              Had had that final moment
        To say a last fond fairwell that
              Would leave your heart content?
To your mother, father, school chum
 or friend that was always there
But now is gone, and missed so much,
 And now you cannot share.....
        Not but memories that still come
              At times you would have been
        Together had they not so rudely
              Left and not to return again.

Perhaps with pen and paper in verse
You can seal a thought to
Those past from your inner circle
Unto "The Great Interlude".
Where you hope they wait for you
to join them by their side
When it's your turn to leave
And take that long, slow ride.
Verse helps me pass the time
And share with them my
Feelings and my emptiness,
That well that comes up dry
After showing such promise, but then
Coming up short by death,
I should have said it earlier but
Did not waste the breath
Because I thought you would never
Leave me alone like this....
Little did I know or expect that
I would come to miss
The time we spent together. but then,
Life is so short and subtle.
Thread upon thread is laid upon
The loom by a swift but sure shuttle.

LITTLE ONE

Walk with me my little one.
    Would you hold your daddy's hand?
Walk with me along this trail
    Until you can understand
The things that I have suffered
    That you could have a life.
So you wouldn't have to struggle
    Until you became his wife.

And you shall do the same
    For the ones that you hold dear.
You'll keep them out of harm's way
    When you shelter them so near
That they think that they will smother
    As they're snuggling in your grasp.
As they're sheltered from the world
    Till you must let go at last.

Then I think that you'll remember
    Just what I have tried to do.
When you look back at your father
    When the little one was you.
You'll see it isn't de ja vu
    or a mystics glimpse of light
But the circle finding its complete
    And things turned out all right.

02-14-0-2001

Loneliness.

Loneliness is as a large steel trap
Whose jaws are very hard to escape
Waiting for any who come near
And whose jaws are always agape

Upon the mind of a soldier it plays
Making his thoughts of home vivid and bright
Making him wonder why he is there
And just why he's having to fight.

And he is filled with the feelings of fruitlessness
As he watches that which he is assigned
With all the numerous and answerless questions
Roving, crawling, moving through his querying mind.

1971

Margaret's Escape

You showed up day after day,
Weeks gone into months and years
Working in the courts and booking
With all your friends and peers.
    And now the time had come
    To leave that all behind
    To hurry out that door
    Before you lose your mind.
        It's crazy to still work there
        That work will never cease
        It's time to just relax.
        You've earned a bit of peace.
You've made your mark in there,
Gained loved and cherished friends,
Who want to leave with you,
When the need for labor ends.
    Some have left some years ago
    Like Bob and Orb and I,
    But you we've not forgot.
    Some friendships never die.
        We'll catch you on the net
        On Facebook and on the phone
        We'll meet you on the street
        But not hardly ever home.
Be gone, and have some fun…
    Find life where it may be…
        Cause now you have the time…
            And now you're really free.

From Kevin Lieby, with love
07-07-2011

A MARVELOUS WORK

I left my home six months ago
To Journey to this land.
To be a servant of the Lord,
A tool in his hand:
I left my home, and all I love
To work this joyous lot.
I found the joy of all this work
The truest joy I sought.

The message that I give the world
Is of one ordained of God
And I would travel to do this work
Over endless tracts of sod.
To share this word with all who dare
To follow every law:
As Paul of old, as he looked up,
And Christ the Lord he saw.

The message is a marvelous church
As it spreads throughout every land
From Nova Scotia's rocky shores
To pacific island sands.
I pray that ye would open up
When we call at your door
And hear the things that God has done,
Restored His church and more.....

1969

Measured,

If love could be
measured,
and it can't
Trying to measure
either of our
loves
Would be as difficult
as trying to measure
the ocean with a
teacup
It would take a good
part of eternity
Let's just try to
use that eternity
together, instead
of trying to
measure or limit
our love for
each other.

1986

MIKE CHECK

Mike Check!
Mike Check!
        You're getting way too loud.
Mike Check!
Mike Check!
        You're sounding like a crowd.
Mike Check!
Mike Check!
        You need to tone it down.
Mike Check!
Mike Check!
        You make the speaker frown.

2012

MISSING BILLIE

On occasion you discover a beautiful jewel
With facets all straight and true
With colors and shades that catch the eye
That holds your attention like glue.

Sometimes that jewel is a special friend
Filling hours with the joy you share.
Lighting up your day with just her smile
Always lovely, and bright, and fair

Billie was always special to us.
She will always be someone we love.
We no longer stand together down here
'cause she's now looking down from above.

We'll miss for now her wonderful smile
And the stunts she used to pull.
The world for us will be emptier now
And some of its brightness more dull

I know she wouldn't want us to cry.
But she knows it just means we care.
We'll look to the sky and smile for her
'cause she's watching us closely from there.

05-25-09

MISSING ONE

in memory of Ken Barton

We spent many years together.
We talked and traded yarns.
We answered many radio calls
To homes, to shops, to farms.
We wore our badges proudly
And did our duties well.
And always helped each other
As we often tripped and fell.
This one time you've stumbled
And we weren't there for you
And you lacked the will to carry on
And felt that friends were few
And you left us feeling empty,
We didn't have a chance
To walk once more beside you
across this great expanse.
And now you walk alone somewhere
Where we here dare not go
For though we think we're wise
There's some things we don't know.
For you cannot return to us
From across the gulf of death.
So we'll stay here behind you
With those who treasure breath.
We'll wonder long if in some way
We could have stayed your hand
And kept you here beside us
For the loss is hard to stand.
But the Sun comes up tomorrow
No matter what we do.
And the sun goes down tomorrow
Then the cycle starts anew.
And so goes on our toil
For it's never ever done
And now there's more than ever,
Our force is missing one.

12-08-2000

MOON RISE

We parked off the edge of the road
      And stood, leaning against the gate
As the last glow of the summer sun
      Signaled that the day had met its fate.
And the sky burst forth stars
      That gave us our only light
As we talked away the hours
      On that warm and peaceful night.
The frogs and insects sang away
      Each one with his own sweet note
That blended sweetly in a symphony
      That to our ears did float.
Then surly from the eastern mount
      There slowly formed that yellow glow
That is the portents of the orb
      That troubles lover's heartstrings so.
The moon soon finds the mountain crest,
      A spot of light, A glowing coal,
An ember rolling over the peak
      Shedding beams to each ones soul.
It grows into a golden dome
      Held tall by trees in silhouette,
Black on gold, The night so clear
      Neither sight nor sound can I forget.
And so soon the moon is full
      And to our eyes doth shed its light
That I find reflected in your eyes
      When viewed upon this quiet night.
It inches up the soft dark night sky
      On its slow journey to the west
With each short minute it will rise
      Above the tall dark mountain crest.
It puts some highlights in your hair
      And color to your cheeks of cream
And makes me want to taste your lips.
      It feels as if we're in a dream.

6-25-00

Musings of a poet

Sit with me upon yon rock
And talk with me, my muse.
Give unto me thy verse
That other poets cannot mock
Or give to me abuse
For I can do no worse
Than I have done before,
In penning rhymes you've given me
That needed be set down.
It wasn't like a chore
As the poems you can see.
They're jewels in your crown.
They are gathered in my books.
Inscribed down on every page,
Dead to the world at large.
Give not to me those looks
You've given others of my age
For not daring to enlarge
The circle to which I expose
The scribbles of my fevered pen.
For we have written much
And the volume simply grows
On whited paper hid from men
Kept back from others touch.
For musings come from deep within,
Too close unto my heart
To share with the stranger.
Yet, do I long to share them
Or at least to some impart
My musings and my anger

For my poems are emotions
Bared nerves and raw feelings
Naked to the reader
Like the magician's potions,
Light that comes forth beaming
He can look within the writer.
And there he sees the truth
For within, poets cannot hide
From the readers eyes
The rhyming songs of youth.
When upon new wings we rode
Or flew across the skies.
Poems need and ought be shared
And to friends they need be bared
For they are fabric of our souls.
Woven close, as if we cared,
That any fault, therein declared,
Would glare like vented coals.
And now my reverend Muse
Inspire my pen to write
Line after line of feelings
In verse, that I can use
To be recorded byte by byte
In bright or subtle rhyming.
For unto this are poets born
To reach with, then turn without
That which grow within the heart.
So write we in the morn',
Until a bell does end this bout
When we have done our part.

07/30/2001

My Bobbi's Verse

I wrote a song to sing to you
When you were but a babe,
To rock you off to slumber land
When daylight colors fade.
For many times I held you
So snugly in my arms
To keep you safe from scary things,
Away from worldly harms.
You grew quickly through the years
From a toddler to a girl.
Always pretty, sometimes shy,
Complexion like a pearl.
Those eyes of yours are always bright
And wide as if in wonder
Taking in the world's joy,
Aglow, like pirates plunder.
I never realized you would grow
Into such a precious teen,
That young men seem to follow,
Entranced, as in a dream.
But remember, in your daddy's eyes,
You're still his little one.
He sees you sleeping in his arms,
You sucking at your thumb.

With a daddy's love

11-15-2001

My Child

Know this, My child,   As I hold you
Fast asleep in my arms
I feel you warm   Against my breast
And feel close to you.
I received you   A short day ago
From your Father's arms
When He sent you   Down to me to
Nurture and to do
The best I can   To teach you that
He is still there
Behind the veil that   Separates God from mortals
For a short while.
You need to learn   Your way by faith,
Though oft you'll err.
You need to seek Him on your own
In times of trial
Till he holds you   Again to His chest
And says to you,
"Well done My child   now. You're home.
Enter, You have life anew."

My Dream

Martin Luther King had a dream. John F. Kennedy had a dream. Both were stopped by lead pellets fired at high velocity by persons who felt that those dreams could become reality.

I put myself to sleep each night dreaming a sort of directed dream. My fantasies are of me doing something that brings me fame or fortune. But as Huck Finn said to Tom, "You can't live a lie."

In the Twelfth Night, Shakespeare said, "Some are born great, Some achieve greatness, and some have greatness thrust upon them."

I went to a party at a friend's home last summer. One of my fellow workers introduced me to his wife saying that I was the one that wrote those moving poems he had shown her. In his praise I knew I had one less dream to fulfill.

Here is one of my dreams.

I'd always wanted to go on a sea voyage. Ever since I read Jack London I wanted to feel the salt spray on my face and feel the heave of the deck and thrust of the wind in the sails.

I happened to be in the right place at the right time. An empty berth on a tall ship on the way to Hawaii. I told them I knew nothing about sailing but I could cook. They told me I would know a lot by the time we arrived. They had a cook but I was welcome to fill the bunk.

So I stand at the mast as we pull away from the dock at old Fort Mason and head for the Golden Gate. The Rock is off to our right, I guess I'll have to learn to call that starboard. We didn't call it that in the army. I know because I used to patrol Fort Mason as an M.P. I've been under the Golden Gate Bridge a half dozen times on a boat before.
But it was always around the base and back to the wharf. This time I'm not coming back for a while. This time I'm not on a ferry or a fishing boat. This is a real adventure.

In my limited baggage all I have is my clothing and my writing material. The pens are the type that write even on wet paper if necessary. Oil base ink, not water based ink, so the ink will not run if it gets wet. I want my words to be safe.

"Kev," a friend hails me from the pilot shack, "Take the wheel while I run down to get some coffee. Just run her with the wind as she lays now. Nothing ahead of us now but a thousand miles of water." I grasp the wheel and feel the tug of the rudder as it forces the boat across the water slightly to the west instead of towards the shore where the wind is heading.

Jack goes below leaving me alone with the sea. A few of the crew are in the aft talking. But I feel the freedom of a man on the sea. Just a few minutes later and Jack is back. "Well," he says, "you didn't run us into anything, did you?"

"No," I concede, "Like you said. Nothing but a thousand miles of water to slice through."

"You'll be an old hand by the time we reach the Islands."

"Well Jack, I'm already getting old but I'll learn this as fast as the kids."

"Not as hard as it used to be. With GPS and computers controlling the lines you don't need to do more that punch in your destination and watch for obstacles. You always loose if you run into the side of a tanker."

"I'll keep my eye out for them," I assured him, "With the computer you really don't need me at the wheel. Do you, Jack?"

"Nope, but it sure feels good to feel the water as it tugs at the wheel. Makes you feel like you're the master of the universe. It'll get old, especially after dark when you have none but the stars to keep you company. But it doesn't get much better than this." And I agree with Jack as we chase the sun across the water. He looks me over, up and down. "You look like you're handling the swells pretty well. I figured you would be a little green around the gills by now."

"I haven't got a record for chumming the fish. A stomach doesn't get this big by being sensitive."

"I hope you still can say that after the first storm." He quips

"I could lose thirty pounds and still be twice the man you are, Skinny." I retort.

"Only on the scales, my friend. Only on the scales." he counters

We chuckle and silence descends as we listen to the sea and the gulls and the creak of the mast.

MY FAVORITE SUMMER
04-24-2000

My favorite summer
My favorite day
My favorite place
My favorite hobby
My favorite pen

An hour from Reno is a place that I consider heaven. When I was young every other summer we traveled the west coast from the redwoods north to the Strait of Juan De Fuca. The other years we camped just sixty miles from home.

We would hook up the little travel trailer that contained an ice box, a water tank that we had to pump water from by hand, beds, and a stove.

We traveled through Bordertown, Chilcoot, Vinton, and Portola. We turned off the main road to the left and passed through GreyEagle. About a mile or two south we took a right and went up hill past Fraizer Falls and up to the Lakes Basin Campground.

We would spend months up in the mountains. An outhouse for a bathroom and the stream for as bathtub. The only time we used soap was for our hands before we ate. Moms are like that.

The campground was a trailhead and a doorway to adventure.

Grassy Lake, shallow and quiet, warmed the swimming hole just below it. The ruins of the old lodge still shows and that makes a neat fort. The rocks on the opposite side of the swimming hole makes a warm towel when heated by the sun. At night it retains the heat of the day to dry you after a swim.

The trail past Grassy Lake leads to a stream that comes from Long Lake far above and it has a falls ending in a pool where lovers try to skinny dip when they think no one is around. The water, cooled by the run down hill from the already cold lake, is almost too cold to swim but it seems a good excuse to take your clothes off.

At the other end of the camp ground is a double trailhead. One trail leads west to Long lake and Mt. Elwell. The trail leads up a steep grade past a huge rock that shades the trail and shadows the snow bank that lasts until late summer. Sliding down it in your cut offs and T-shirt is a great diversion on a warm summer day. A summer snowball fight is an excellent adventure. Climbing up on the rock you can bombard unwary hikers as they pass. But who would think of such a thing?

A mile up the trail and we crest a rise and see Long Lake with Mt. Elwell rising up on the other side like a huge granite wall. Only the adventurous or the crazy like me make our way between the peak and the lake. One slip and you slide hundreds of feet down the sheer granite face and into the shockingly cold and clear waters only a mountain top lake could have. But sense of adventure often overrules common sense and more than once I've made the perilous transverse without rope or climbing shoes.

Most of the time I bear left of the Mt. Elwell trail and take the easy trail to Silver Lake. We boys used to skinny dip here before they paved the road to the camp ground and thereby let city people crowd the locals out.

If you turn right here you go up to the Pacific Crest Trail. If you turn left here you go down the trail from lake to lake. Big Bear Lake, Little Bear Lake, and Cub Lake line up below Silver Lake. The trail splits and one goes back to the trailhead and camp. The other goes past a lodge and to Gold Lake.

I don't know anything about the Girl Scout Camp on Gold Lake. I don't know the way back in the dark without a flashlight to give away our position. I don't know any holes back in the manzanita where you can hide until the tent councilors give up looking for you. The sheriff couldn't track us on the rock and there wasn't any proof. Anyway there's a statute of limitation isn't there?

My memories of the whole area are green and granite. The trails I can still find and they take me to the memories of my youth. To old friends that no longer visit and to a cousin that yearly makes the hike with me into our yesterdays. We sit resting at places along the trail that we used to scurry past. But now we rest and take the trail at a slower pace. We talk of adventures, of blazing our own trails to cut between lakes. We talk of forts and strongholds we built of rocks and limbs and our Indian wars waged with sticks and water balloons. Our later wars weren't all that fun.

Our only foes then were mosquitoes and the sunburns along with the occasional black bear and wasp. But our usual banter and laughter kept the bears away and the cool mud took away the stings.

We were invincible in the warm summers of youth. And our energy wasn't limited by our years as it is now. But my hour is almost up and I'm sad because if I'd grabbed my keys instead of my pen I would be in the pines and the cool mountain air instead of just writing these lines. My feet would be in the pool by the trail and I would again be in my favorite place reliving my youth.

04-24-2000

My life defined

My life right now can be defined
By the contents of my right front seat.
You may ask why am I defined
By an empty bucket seat of a car.
It's not empty at all I would respond.
It's just not occupied by a person
It is full of papers, Sun Glasses
And a couple of audio tapes.
And it says to the world
Here is a lonesome man.
He uses the passenger seat
Of a muscle car as a catch all.
He doesn't fill it with the posterior
Of a fine looking young lady.

I drive alone into the night
And I listen to the radio
Or to the tapes that I have
Strewn around the seats of my car.
The papers there and there
Are poems that I write alone
In the solitude of my home
For I am alone there, also.
And maybe that is the way
That I was meant to be,
Alone, with no one to blame
Except for the pride in my heart.

I can’t find someone who could
Just tolerate me for a while.
My time is spent before the television,
At work, or doing nothing,
Because if I stop to feel,
All I feel is the hurt
Of the times I let someone
Get close to me for once
And I disappoint them somehow
And end up alone and hurt again
Most of the time not knowing why
But full of hurt and pain.

Sometimes I feel like a leper
Warning people away from me
Lest they too bear the scars
And scabs of the hurts that seems
Be my lot in this existence.
BACK AWAY AND MAYBE I WON’T GET HURT.
Like all the others who seem to afflict me
By trying to come too close.
Flee while you can. Can’t you see
The scars of the times I’ve tried?

04/14/2002

MY HELPER

Men, Here we are in the army.
Not by our choice, I know
But because some guy in Washington
Said, "It's your time to go."
Now we're doing things we never anticipated.
Learning to kill and inflict pain,
Learning the ways of warfare,
Learning to stand in the rain.
Why must a people of peace
Learn such horrid and bloody ways
That might remain in our minds
And hinder us all our days.
I feel trapped in the army
Like an animal in a cage
And I know you do too
And at your prime of age.
I don't pretend to have all
The answers of army life
How to make the best of it
Or how to avoid its strife.
But I know this one thing
Which helps me all the time.
We have One to rely on,
My thoughts to Him incline.
God is the One to rely on,
Who helps me in time of need.
He helps me in my every act,
My every thought and deed.
His help has given me solace
And peace within my mind
An inspiration to give me
Strength in deeds of every kind
I wish more men find this help,
This strength could help them out
This force could transform their lives.
(Of this I have no doubt.)
So think on this, you army men.
Can you use a help like this?
Can you find a way to God?
Can you really afford to miss?

1971

Ode to a dingle ball

For the AC4 staging crew
(Sometimes inspiration is right
in front of your eyes)

Oh, dingle ball
Thou butthole lint
Wad of cotton
With brownish tint.

Strong of smell
And little fame
I sometimes wonder
Whence thou came.

Why growest thou
On anal hair
Where others shun,
That sideways stare?

You're seldom seen
And never felt.
Why growest thou
Below the belt?

Can you tell
What lothesome purpose
You gather on
The buttock's surface?

11/21/06

ODE TO A DISASTER

We've seen those clips played over and over
As if we could ever forget
The day that rained terror from the sky
And the dust hasn't settled yet.

The death toll seems to wax and ebb
Just like the moon and tide.
And I start to think we'll never know
The full number who have died.

They worked in towers as warm and safe
As any one could be.
A hundred stories of both steel and glass
Once stood beside the sea.

But as the dreams of mice and men
Often tumble to the ground
So did these sentinels of world trade
Turn to rubble all around.

The finest of New York were called and came
They were heroes to the last
And hundreds of them were called to pay
By the reapers fiery blast.

And thousands dug for weeks on end
To see who they could save,
But sadly there were but a few
That didn't find a grave.

Their loved ones searched in vain for them
For those they loved and missed.
They checked hospitals, and streets, and friends,
For their names upon some list.

And some there are that won't be found
With nothing left to bury.
Their names will be cut in sheets of stone
Just etched into our memory.

Most of us have shed many a tear
And burned a mourning candle.
And seen the grief across the land.
It's more than some can handle.

But life goes on for those who live
Just like it did before,
Except for threats, and rants, and raves
That what we need is war.

I've done that war thing once before
And I didn't find it fun.
I spent three years away from here
Packing ammo and a gun

And in the end both sides had lost
A lot more than just time.
I thought we learned a lot from that.
Is not its wall a shrine?

What we don't want now is more body bags
Filled and draped with flags
And parents with their dreams all cold,
More children missing dads.

We need to cool our heels a bit.
We need justice, Not revenge!
We need to do what's right for once
'Cause it matters how it ends.

Let's take a deep and cleansing breath,
Step back and get perspective.
Let's hear the counsels of the wise,
Not shout and hurl invectives.

Let's do it right and do it smart,
Not run in half prepared.
We want our armies safe at home
While our enemy runs scared.

09/17/2001

ODE TO THE PHALLICALLY CHALLENGED

If a poet can't get lucky
It's his pen that isn't sharp
For he cannot write the verses
That can touch a woman's heart

Sure he's full of pains and rages
Which he puts in words and lines
But it's words of love that stirs her up
And he turns her off with whines.

His useless tool hangs flaccidly.
Could it be erectile failure?
He may as well be not endowed
For his lack of a woman's favor.

He should be called "Tim Go Without"
For all the luck he's had
And he sports a rotten haircut,
And his body odor's bad.

He cruises chicks without success,
They all just turn away
They find him so repulsive
That dogs, with him, won't play.

He may, some day, change his ways
And he'll learn how love is made.
Until then, he can go without
And be known as "Tim Not Laid"

09/05/2002

ON LISTENING TO JAZZ

Jazz crashes over me like a warm wave
Drowning out the babble of the loud bar
And transporting me into the land of music
Driven there by the drums, sax and guitar.

Finding my feet tapping to the rhythm
And my body swaying to the beat.
And the girls out there dancing
Seem to be driven by their feet.

People shout to others over their drinks.
And people mill around talking to friends
Juggling their glasses and bottles
Drowning their cares with elbow bends.

But I just listen to the music
That's driven and amplified past me
To the laughing and talking crowd.
I wonder -- do they not enjoy the energy.

You can't enjoy jazz while talking.
You must let it capture your soul.
You feel it more than you hear it,
Warm and bright like a coal.

But they're the ones that are missing
Stirring music put out by the band
To the ears of those that enjoy it
And when done we give them a hand.

01-20-2002

ON THE PICTURE OF A BOY ON A ROCK

The days are long when the days are warm.
I sit and watch the cold water swirl and splash.
I feel the cool heavy air on my bare leg.
I smell the grass which grows behind my back
And the flowers right there smell as sweet as mommy.

I want to play and splash among the damp rocks
To wet my socks and shoes, pants and shirt,
To feel the cool wet against my warm skin.
But dad is watching so close I wouldn't dare.
I have to behave like a gentleman for this picnic.

Just because dad's boss asked us to come
And play with the other kids of the office workers.
But I found my special place at this creek
The bigger kids can hog the swings and toys
The younger toddle or crawl on their blankets.

But I can sit and watch the water flow
And listen to the babble all by myself.
I wonder if there are any fish hiding down there
With their brown backs and bellies of silver
Making them so hard to see from up here.

But I sit on my rock like a gentleman
And feel the sun on my face and arms
And hear the other kids laugh and yell
When I want to be alone playing in the water
Instead of being a good boy for daddy's boss.

06/01/2001

On the Santa Cruz Boardwalk

07-24-2001

Have you ever sat on the benches on The Santa Cruz Boardwalk and looked out over the sea? I can ignore the pressing hoards of fun seekers, the sounds of the rides, and the begging gulls. I feel the beat of the sun upon my body and I know even with the sun block I will burn somewhere I missed.

Today there is a wall of clouds out on the water. It looks like a stationary Tsunami standing out in Monterey Bay. How far out you cannot tell. Or how high and dense you cannot tell. But the two brown spots, one big and one small, that look like islands sticking out of the fog are actually high points on the Monterey Peninsula or so I am told by someone who knows the bay better than I. I will have to take their word for it because for my eyes tell me they are islands, but eyes can be fooled by fog, even a good distance.

There are sails on the water. I watch as a group of five cut their way out, back, and across the bay. They are single masted, white sailing craft. One is larger than the others. They look like they are in a race or regatta. Maybe it's some sort of a sailing school practicing, cutting their paths across this edge the Pacific.

I am treated to the soaring of pelicans, the Spanish alcatraz, crossing the scene with their massive wings and their breasts like keels of feathered ships. They look so noble and stalwart as they glide in search of the fish near the surface upon which to feed. A local points them out as a point of interest. I tell her we have them in Nevada. She questions me and I tell here about the grounds the birds have on Pyramid and Anaho islands out in Pyramid Lake where they are protected by law for their breeding and nesting.

I look at the sand in front of the boardwalk. It has a course of water cutting it in half, slashing across to the right diagonally. I'm told it is where a small river empties into the ocean. It reminds me that this area is the interface between the fresh water land and the salty ocean, between the beasts of the land and the beasts of the sea.

Maybe the thing that enthralls us with beaches is that interface between the known and the unknown. I read that we have only explored five percent of the oceans. I wonder, do we fear the rest because we don't understand it? I don't even understand what I see now.

ONCE AGAIN OUR BADGES

For Officer Mike Scofield
Killed in the line of duty 09/26/2002

Once again our badges hang
      With a band that says we mourn.
And once again the pipes will play
      And a flag draped casket borne.
Uniformed files of Blue and Green.
      The Honor Guards in Black,
In our formal ranks we stand
      In tie, in coat, and hat.
And his widow weeps in dignity
      And his children's tears are cold
As they listen to his eulogy.
      He was good, and fair, and bold.
He wore his badge with honor
      And he did what he was asked
And he died while he was rolling
      To yet another task.
So many times we've seen it
      Over the course of years
But it never gets any easier
      To stifle back the tears.
We called this man a brother
      For a badge hangs on our chests
Be it shaped like a shield or a star
      It signifies the best.
We're proud that he was one of us.
      We'll not forget his name.
His legend will live on in us.
      We will never be the same.

ONCE WE STOOD

Once we stood shoulder to shoulder
Each in armor, with badge and gun
We shared our watch in the dark of night
And we shared our time in the sun.

We shared the load in the good times
And the bad times we finally got past.
We thought we'd grow old together
But more than one of us didn't last.

Some partners and buddies have fallen.
Laid low by the rigors of life
And were claimed by the infamous Reaper
In his cowl with his sickle-like knife

And now you wander those shadows
Away from our hearing and sight
Until we all join at the Judgment
When we're chosen to stand at His right.

Then we'll sit and tell the old stories
In heaven they'll know they're all true
And we'll stop and laugh at the rookies
Though they're no longer young and so new.

I'm sure we'll all be together
'Cause we paid the price here on Earth
When we walked the thin line together
And knew the beats and our turf.

03/17/2003

OUR HAUNTED JAILS

More people die in jail than just about anywhere else in our society. Whether by their own hands, by drug withdrawal, by alcohol toxemia, or by the results of self abuse, the death toll rises as the jail ages.

Spirits of those who expire in the chains of society haunt the chambered halls of that jail. So often Correctional Officers are startled by movement just beyond their field of vision. So often They look for the source of the noise or movement and find it came from nowhere, or did it come from anywhere?

The high anxiety and stress that occurs in the custodial setting emanates from the deaths of those who died with their grievous sins upon their souls. Denied the rites of clergy and not having the chance to pay the price of justice they are forever bound by the chains forged by their acts as surely as Christopher Morley in Dicken's Christmas Carol .

Can you imagine the weight of the chains these lost souls drag through the corridors of this nations jails? No wonder cops are stereotyped as paranoid. They are burdened by the specters of these deaths.

Those officers who are forced to kill an offender in the line of duty are also burdened knowing they caused a sinning man to die without confessing his sins to God. More links are formed in the spectral bondage of souls in the jail.

I watched helplessly as a man died from substance withdrawal as our medical staff struggled to save his life and he cursed God and me as he succumbed to alcohol induced seizure which stopped his heart. Upon his lips was the promise to come back and haunt us for withholding the life sustaining alcohol from him. His curse and his burdened soul walks the halls of the jail and my mind each night.

The crimes and sins against society get worse each day. These criminals, dying in their sins, will ever haunt the halls of justice and the minds and hearts of their families and their jailers.

04-10-00

PAPER PAGES

05-22-00

I look at what’s in my room for an Item
      about which I can build a scene;
The Books,   The pictures,
The stereo,   The empty plate,
The computer.
My eyes fasten on the one Item
      that I as a writer focus so much attention.
Boxes of paper,   Filler paper,
meeting pads,   note books,
computer paper,   Steno pads,
Theme books,   scratch pads.
These precious sheets of pulverized pine;
These luscious layers of lined cellulose;
These white wafers of writing wonderment.
Isn’t the goal of us all here
      to fulfill our fantasies with finely filled flat folios.
We may have books filled with other peoples dreams in our
      library
but we as writers want to produce that great, gregarious,
      gargantuan, golden tome.
The one that will be remembered a thousand years as the
      paramount pinnacle of pleasure reading.
The best selling book that brought big bucks and bright
billings.
To strike the keys of my computer,
      or draw with pen the words across the page.
To pass to another this way the wondering of my mind.
To make another feel the wanton wonder of wild abandon of a
      moment of my time.
To fasten in the ink the beauty of the full moon resting on
the   mount in the morning at the moment that it makes
contact.

To describe the pastels of that moment so all the lovers of the world can imagine the image intimately.
To be the definition of descriptive dalliance by delineating
daringly the devised dissertations of the writer.
To be recognized in the crowd as one apart,
who can place his heart
upon the chart of the writers art.
To break all the writing rules,
because they are just tools,
to be followed by fools,
who know nothing of the jewels,
that can be found in the writers mind.
Methinks that many millions of modern Miltons
think meanly of their musings
because the artless write the textbooks
that try to tell them to follow rules.
Break the mold,
warm the cold
get a volume sold
the words upon this page
will travel past our age
and puzzle a future sage,
About what I really meant
when completing this assignment.

PICTURE IN MY HAND

Darling, I gaze at this picture of you,
and I see the object of all my dreams,
The object of all that I hope for.
You'll never know just how much it means.

I love you, darling, More than I express:
More, I think, than words can ever convey.
I want you to know this love too,
That we might share it day by day.

I feel that we can make love work'
Not for now, but forever, side by side.
We can be together always in this love,
For it is a love none can hide.

I think of you now as I stare
At this picture of you in my hand
Yearning for the time we'll be together
Praying the time to be close at hand.

1970

POEMS

Poems are always there.
They are a sticky black glue
Pushed into a thin tube
Held back by a ball that'll move

The soul of a poet seeks
To bring the poem from the
Tube to the paper of white
Making the glue flow so smooth

With the words that are the poem
Flowing in the black and white
Making the paper sing the
Song that pleases the Muse.

7/95

POEMS - BLOOD, PAIN, INK

Poems are not written
            They are Born,
Borne of pain, a poet
            Who does not hurt
Cannot write, such is
            The heart of a poet.
And it is that soft part
            That hurts, for poems
Come from the heart.

Perhaps this is why a poet
            Loves, for love is born
Of pain, and poems are
            Born of pain, so poems
Are borne of love.

A poem is not written in ink,
            It is written in blood
For blood is the ink of the heart.
            The blood of a poet yearns
To spill upon the paper of life
            To find the words to express the
Pain, so all can share the love
            And the pain of the poet.

11-16-95

POET, POET

Poet, Poet, Grasp thy pen
And write a song for me.
Write it on a whitened sheet
Made from a noble tree.

Poet, Poet, spread thy ink.
Scribble words upon a line.
Write it neat and quickly.
I want the thing to rhyme.

Poet, Poet, pierce my heart
With words that make me cry.
When I lay this paper down
I'll do it with a sigh.

Poet, Poet, pen the words
That I, myself, would write
If I but had a poet's gift
His vision and his sight.

Poet, Poet make my poem
To touch my lover's heart.
Make her feel the way I feel
For she's lovely and she's smart.

Poet, Poet, bare my soul
Which I could never do,
For I hide things deep inside me
Not out in front, like you.

Poet, Poet, I'll post away
Those cherished words you pen.
A card unto my lady love
To bring her back again.

Poet, Poet, I envy you.
You have the words to say,
To make the ladies love you.
You sweep their hearts away.

Poet, Poet, Why sit you there
In your dwelling all alone?
If you but write a lady
She'll make that house a home.

Poet, Poet, reach you out
And take your lover's hand
And with sweet words awaken her.
You'll together walk the sand.

Poet, Poet, take some time,
See it trickle down the glass.
Feel the rhythm of the waves,
The moments as they pass.

Poet, Poet, I see you now,
That you've chosen oft to write
Quietly behind your doors
And oft late into the night.

Poet, Poet, Know we need
The words just you can say.
Illuminate our hearts for us,
Make sunshine from the gray.

Poet, Poet, Give us pause,
For you write just what we feel.
A poet's pen, A poet's heart
Can tell us what is real.

Poet, Poet, sit you down
And call upon your Muse
And know the verses that you write
Can only be The Blues.

02/26/2001

POLLUTED MAINE

The rivers once were clean and nice
The waters so clean and pure
The air crisp and always fresh
With room to "fish and fur".

Green trees and grasses were everywhere
Its glories we'd loud proclaim;
For all know this once described
The great green State of Maine.

But rivers now are brown and dead.
No longer will they freeze
And if you even walk nearby
You'll catch some dread disease.

They're so thick with foamy crowns
That it makes your stomach churn.
They've turned to what is best described
As an enormous funeral urn.

The mountains have been stripped of trees
To make great rolls of paper.
So now the once green hills are called
About ten thousand "Hell's half acres".

And yet we let this rape go on
And don't even try to stop it
For the paper makes those dollar signs
And even that more important credit.

Pretty soon old Maine will surely die,
The cesspool of the east,
For it will no longer keep alive
A man or fly or beast.

1970

THE PRAYER OF A POET

My heart breaks every time they award the Nobel Prize for Literature and my name is not listed.
Sorry babe, A man has to have his fantasies, and they're not all about you.
I know that in your mind you always come before anything else.
But there are some thing that even you can't do.

I want my name remembered for what I write.
I want my name carved into the marble above the library door.
I want lovers to read my words to each other.
I want my books on the best seller lists, and more.

I want to be quoted in class like Chaucer and Shakespeare.
I want to be asked for my autograph when I'm having dinner.
I want to be introduced to famous people as "the noted poet"
I want people to know my name, and remember me thinner.

Is it too much to ask to be loved by the masses?
Am I trying to take too much pride in my work?
I only ask for a small part of heaven
And I'll try not to act like a jerk.

I write poetry that is really good most the time.
I bring tears to the eyes of some readers
As they read the verses that flow from my pen.
So recognition is not more than I deserve

Look at my poems, My little rhymes, my verses
Do they not stir your heart and moisten your eyes
Do they not tweak those feelings way down deep
And make the hidden emotions within you rise.

Hear my words. Examine the songs of my heart.
Listen to the rhythm, the meter, the grief,
That I try to convey across the gulf to you
That you may read and feel and find relief.

For I write that you may know my heart.
That you may feel what I feel when I write
That you can see, as I see, when writing
These words of mine late in the night.

I want to be the world's poet, not just me.
I want to leap into the sky and fly on wings of flame.
I want to be the remembered poet, "A bard",
I just want people to remember my name.

12-10-2001

PSALM OF SUCCOR

God stretches forth his hand   But do I reach to meet Him?
        Do I seek His counsels? Or do I rely on my own arm?
Do I make the effort To look away from sin
        Or do I see how close I can come to it without harm?

Only I can kneel And therefore put out my hand
        To receive his proffered Help to heal my wounded heart.
Only He can give The strength I need to stand
        Against the worldly storms That lash my home and hearth

Reach forth to God And live. Reach forth in prayer.
        Ignore the worlds limits. What are limits to a Being
Who possesses all power. Who knows all, and is always there?
        Limits are the chains man and Satan in his scheming.

Prayer to a Father Who knows his children's needs
        As we know needs Of the children of our flesh.
Comfort - found in arms Enfolded, we can sleep
        The sleep of children So in need of rest

The rest of God, The solace free from stress,
        The quietness of peace After the worldly storms has passed
And left its wake of tattered souls, and yes
        A few but sheltered By His hand from the blasts.

Shelter me, My God, Put Thy arms about and hold
        My heart to Thine through the trials of the day.
Enfold me, I pray. Don't let the night be cold
        And chill my soul But let me by Thy hearthstone stay.

1988?

PTSD and VA

Why don't you treat me?
I've been to your damn classes.
Wipe it, take away my rage,
Return me to the masses!
Give me the right tools
To heal and to cope.
Return me back to "Normal",
Restore me to my hope.

I have seen too much horror
And felt so much pain.
I've witnessed and I've suffered
Now I'm classified "insane."
I have open wounds in my soul
And I weep and I cry.
I have loosened all my demons
And still I wonder … why?

Your pills do not calm me,
I still rage and I storm
And I find that my emotions are
Far from the "social norm".
You sit behind your polished desk
And question and you write …
But why are you not helping me …
Can't you see I'm wound up tight?

I struggle to remain afloat
And all you do is talk
Instead of tossing me a rope
You heave a big old rock.
I think that I'll just walk away
And find my own solution.
It's not like I could find some help
In this blasted institution.

02/02/2012

PURPOSE

I look out of this window and
I see freedom.
Freedom to do those things
We really wish to do.
Knowing that as long as we do
not infringe
Upon the rights of others, Our
Freedoms will continue.
Yet we become, upon infringing
upon another's rights
Unworthy of the freedoms which
We do now possess
And hence are punished by a revocation
Of these rights
And any other just, and applicable
Form of redress.
Thus our occupation as enforcers and protectors
Of this freedom
Becomes necessary as justified by both
Deduction and reason.

1971

QUEST FOR ETERNITY

The Moon rises over the hills,
No longer a virgin of dreams.
So long have men yearned for her
And around her built their schemes.

The moon has been wantonly touched
And has fallen from her majesty.
Once untouched by all of mankind
Now has been violated by humanity.

Like a woman stripped of her virtue
She lies in remorse and shame,
But to those who understand her
She will always be the same.

Though of rocks and not blue cheese,
Though her mystery has been disclosed,
She's the symbol of those the world over,
Of which the true meaning none knows.

For she inspired all men's dreams
And caused them to bear their humility
Built by the awe of her vastness
(Of her place in the eternities).

Men, who aspired to the heights unknown
To lead a world forth from contentment
And send them hurling through space
To a time when dreams find success.

But what have we now to dream on???
THE STARS that shine in infinity
To send beyond her our dreams.
Yes! This is the quest of humanity.

1969

A QUIET DAY

I woke up late this morning
To the smell of an autumn rain
The wind blew down some apples
And changing weather brought some pain

Dogs barked as I got my paper
Still more as I raised my flag.
News told of the bombs in Kabul
Cruise Missiles hit Jalalabad.

But my morning was pretty normal
Sunlit clouds obscured the skies
I ate a cream cheesed bagel
Rubbed the sleep from out my eyes.

I was freshened by my shower
Morning hygiene, and a shave.
Used the vacuum, did some sweeping,
Straightened up my hermits cave.

Then I sat and did some reading,
And had to shake myself awake
For I had drifted into slumber
So my lunch was getting late.

I warmed up my Sanyo big screen,
Watched a movie while I ate.
Wrote some lines upon this paper,
Nothing special, Nothing great.

Then it's off to hear some poets
Reading late into the night.
This life can't get much better.
At least for me it seems all right.

10-08-2001

QUESTIONS

Have you ever thought of God this way
That he is just a man
That He is like unto a general
The world at his command.

That he works through laws of nature
More higher than those of earth
And in order to have gone so far
He had suffered mortal birth.

Is there a Mother in Heaven with Him,
An exalted Heavenly Wife,
That through this birth in heaven
We gained our heavenly life.

These questions are all unanswered
To those of us who care
But if we live with him again
We'll find the answer there.

1970

Reaction

She reads my poem,
And I see tears
Growing in her eyes.
I know she feels
That which I felt
When penning those lines.

Is that the mark
Set by a poet
For which he tries?
To write the tears.
His heart to yours
Set forth in rhymes.

Feel what I feel.
See through my eye
That which I see.
Reach with my hand,
To grasp the pen,
To spread the ink,

To share with you,
Tears of my heart.
Let them flow free
Onto this paper white
Form with tender care
A poet - reader link.

01-29-2001

RESTORED CHURCH

A Small Voice whispers to me
Thou hast a work to do.
A message sweet It gave to me
To deliver unto you
To tell you of a prophet of God
Called a hundred years ago.
Who three million people hold in laud
With seeds of Good to sow.

By your fruits ye shall know,
For better, or for worse,
And the seeds that they sow
As I write in this verse.
They are growing the fastest
Among churches of men.
Their work is The Master's
To all they're a friend.

Their members all do work
With all of their might
And never do shirk
For their goal is in sight.
They sing with one accord
Their voices flow like fountains
And they worship the Lord
From the high rocky mountains.

This word they all share
To all upon the earth
To all who would dare
To believe in its worth
The true Christian love
Can be found without flaw
It's restored to the earth
As the prophets foresaw.

1969

SECRETARIES' DAY

Day after day, week after week,
We don't appreciate all you do,
The endless chores, notes you keep,
Records filed of business old and new,

The endless hours you sit there
At a desk and a phone.
We couldn't do it on a dare.
We couldn't make it on our own.

You organize everything in your reach
And smooth the office rough edge.
You print and collate, type the speech
And grow flowers on the ledge.

You remind us of our every stop,
Of the date, the hour, the time.
Where the meeting notes were kept,
Where to initial, and what to sign.

We never notice those little things
We take for granted every day,
How many times the dang phone rings
Or listen to what you say.

Just once a year we recognize
A day named just for you.
Just on secretaries day we realize
The importance of what you do.

SIERRA NEVADA SUNSET

My favorite color is somewhere
Between the orange and grays
Of a Nevada sunset

When those wafty lines say
That over there somewhere
Someone's getting wet.

And in the coolness of the
Spring evening people walk
In the quiet neighborhood.

Not for exercise but to enjoy
Relief from the day's heat.
It's restful and feels good

And you meet friends out walking
For the same reasons.
Talking, hand in hand.

For the hush has reached
Out to all of us
So blessed in this land.

The sweet smell of the wildflowers
Caresses our senses out of
The dark openness

As the warm Sierra night
Touches all of us and seems
To make us restless.

06-29-95

SMALL THINGS

Have you ever thought of the small things.
    The things that you ofttimes do.
The things that make you a special one.
    The things that make you you

    Small things that grow into a big
And are shown to us each day.
    A mighty oak sprung from a twig.
A small thing, so they say.

Yes, It's the little things that make big
    It's the small things, like the cell
That make up the creation called you.
    Such artistry makes my heart swell.

1970

SMALLER

Somehow the old house doesn't look as big as it did back when I was growing up. The blocks of the old neighborhood shrink as the years go by too. But walking them tires you out now more quickly because you weigh four times what you did in your youth.

We used to think we were brave paratroopers when we were jumping from the top bunk to the floor with a blanket clutched tightly in each fist. Or adventurers when we climbed the front of the dresser carefully so it wouldn't fall over on top of you.

If you tried to climb the trees you climbed in your youth you would tear the limbs off like Alley Oop, as if anyone born in the last forty years would know who Alley Oop was.

Do you remember walking along the rails with arms extended out to your sides, foot in front of foot, as long as you could keep your balance. Or crawling through the hobo jungle by the ditch near the tracks and coming across places that someone had slept last night after he jumped from a slow moving train. We would play for hours in areas we would not allow our children to play in because they are too dangerous.

Remember playing on the roof of the neighbor's chicken coop. The strong smell of guano drying in the warm summer sun.

Remember building a snow ramp in the back yard and standing on your sled holding the rope in one hand and surfing down the hardened, frozen surface and taking the curve with bravado and cheers that you survived.

Did you jump from the irrigation pipe into the bigger ditch below that wasn't deep enough to break your fall. Then did you limp for the next month like a lame horse because you bruised your foot so badly that it would barely hold you weight.

We were always in a little trouble but rarely in a lot of trouble. I guess we were just normal boys, whatever that means, growing up in a small town in the sixties. We didn't have much, but we could entertain ourselves and the other neighborhood kids with sticks for guns and brooms for horses. Our mom used to punish us by taking away our pop guns but plain sticks could be machine guns, grenade launchers or sniper rifles or even a "one man army gun" that the rich kids could afford.

Life seemed a lot simpler then. You were not concerned with anybody but yourself and whomever was around to play with.

Cut off pants (that were cut off because the holes in the knees were too big to patch), T-shirts, and old gym shoes (tennis shoes were high class toys) were all you wore six days a week. Sunday you had to wear your best clothes to Church but when you got home you could escape again into the careless clothes of the adventurer.

The fields and fences to the west gave you room to explore and burn off the weight of your mom's cooking. It didn't make any difference if the land was owned by the state and posted with warning signs and fenced with barbed wire. If Mr. Brownie caught you in the haystacks you were really were in for it. But if you stayed in the open, he couldn't sneak up on you and he wasn't fast enough to overtake you in the flight of sheer terror.

We spent hours, indeed days, playing by the trees in the fields. The small irrigation ditches that flooded the fields formed islands that you could step to or jump to and you could sit against the trees in their shade and just listen to the water flowing by. It drowned out the noise of town and you were kind of in the world all alone. The ground was moist and left the seat of your pants damp, but in the heat of the summer sun it would dry as soon as you got up and moving.

We were always moving, going to, coming from, or planning the conquest of the world. Forts were dug in an empty lot with a roof of an old pallet and some card board as roofing. We camouflaged it with a layer of dirt and stuck some sticks and bushes into it to make it invisible to someone not looking. We had learned the skill by watching John Wayne. His movies were great training films. We gladly shared the fort with spiders and the lizards that ate them. Squirrels moved into them as soon as we left.

Those magnifying glasses out of your Cracker Jacks took care of the ants that came around. We just focused the sun on them and heard them snap with steaming death. But if you didn't watch where you stand its brothers would bite your legs in the instant retribution of Karma.

The alley was the kid's expressway. Grown ups used the paved streets. The alley was used each week by the garbage truck but the rest of the week it belonged to us. You didn't have to watch for cars. If you did encounter one you heard it crunching the gravel long before it was near. It was simply our short cut to every other kid's house in the area. And it was lined with those cans full of treasures that were always of value to kids if you got to them before the garbage man.

Every yard had a shed on or near the alley, with roofs to play on and windows to climb through when hiding. There were also pets to pester that made their home in those sheds. I don't remember ever taking anything from those sheds. But we knew where everything in the neighborhood was, where to borrow a tire pump or who had patches for your tubes.

Those tubes were used in the river on the other side of the farm to the west. Or in the ditches if you kept an eye out for leeches. We even took the bus to the other side of town. Filled our deflated tubes at a tire shop and floated back home in that river. We could catch a ditch from the diversion dams and float within two blocks of the house. We had to wear our old gym shoes in the river when tubing. Drunks and kids threw bottles in the river and then practiced hitting them with rocks. If you didn't wear shoes you could cut your feet.

That river was also the source of many a wonderful fish fry. My cousin would come over and spend the night. We would go after nightfall to gather worms. The giant worms called nightcrawlers infested the lawn of a neighbor and we harvested them often. The next day at dawn we would walk across the farm and spend the morning drowning worms. Most the time we caught our limits of rainbow trout and we cleaned them right on the banks before we walked home. We cleaned them with our pocket knives.

They were ubiquitous. No self respecting boy over ten would be caught without his pocket knife. They were not fancy knives. Just a couple of blades and a screw driver/can opener. They were sturdy because we were country kids not city kids. You carried them to school and to church and to scouts. They meant you were trusted by your parents and other adults. They were tools, not weapons. Every kid could gut a fish in a minute with a pocket knife. Most of us also had hunting knives that we took to scout camp and camping trips.

Things have changed since the house grew smaller. Just maybe I remember the good things from a simpler, quieter time.

03/23/2001

SNOWS OF SPRING

My squeaking decorative windmill
      Tells me of the wind
Blowing down from the Sierras
      To my high valley home.
The brightness of the curtains
      Tells me one more tale
Of spring snow upon my
      Quickly greening lawn.
The coolness of my bedroom
      Tells me of the frost
That again has nipped the buds
      Of my poor apple trees.
Most years only the shape
      Of the many leaves
Tell me that some year
      They will grow fruit
And that the fruit will be
      Called an apple.
I know again why, in Reno,
      We store our winter clothes
In June instead of April,
      Like they do in Vegas.
We live in the mountains
      Where our air is clear
And though some days are warm
      We keep a jacket near.

04-03-2001

SOAR ALOFT

A bird glides in the wind
Riding the updrafts and soaring
Above the land.

He faces the oncoming storm
As it approaches. Cresting the
Far away mountains.

This causes the wind that allows him
To soar. Flying with just the effort
Of controlling wings.

Back and forth above the small hill
Using its lift to be one
With the wind.

We also must soar in the face of
The storm, Finding uplift in its gusts
By spreading our wings.

Can we find control in the tips
Of our wings? Can we lift and glide
With hardly any effort?

We can try and learn to soar in
The winds of life; held aloft by
Invisible strength from below.

Held aloft by pressures of the storm
Itself controlled by the heart and mind
Like a bird.

01-11-98

The Sound of Bombers

I heard a Bomber today
     And I didn't have to hide
I did not have to go to a shelter
     Or cower somewhere inside

I did see smoke in the air
     And I watched as the fire units passed
But I did not hear bombs explode
     Or fear that this was my last.

Because bombers here fight fires
     For I live in the U. S. of A
And sirens mean help is on the way
     Not hide for the rest of the day

I take for granted my peace
     And I pay the taxes to pay those
Who fly bombers over my house
     Or man the fire hose.

I do not fight flames myself
     But I call friend, those who do
And I can rely on them
     That man the fire crew.

I cheer the man in yellow turnouts
     And under his helmet I see a grin
For he knows how to fight that fire
     And he knows he will win.

And he faces the heat and smoke
     Sometimes with just shovel and axe
And we buy him food and water
     To cool him as he attacks

The flame way up there
     Coming down the distant hill
Before it gets near my house
     Where the fires on the grill.

I cheer that firefighter
     I cheer the bombers flight
As they suppress the fire
     That threatens us tonight.

Kevin Lieby

SPRING SNOWS

The wind and snow of a Sierra Spring
      Barely cover the grass, just green
That made it through the winter brown
      But enjoys the moisture that comes down.

Only tulips show their blooms stretched high
      Above the snow their colors fly
In contrast to the sheet of white
      Stretching high they seek the light.

The snow hangs upon the cherry blooms
      But they won't last, they've come too soon,
And so this year will bear no fruit
      And this year nourish just leaf and root.

04/22/2003

STILL BELIEVE

Maybe it's the poet in me
That allows me to still believe in love.
After all, besides all the burns I've suffered,
I still believe in matches.

Each time I find a woman
That finds an interest in me
I throw caution to the wind
And I pursue the relationship.

The flash of her eyes
The flash of her thighs
And the promise of things to come
And my heart is gone.

And they say I'm old enough
To know better,
But better than what?
I've never found anything better.

And I loose myself in her eyes
And she folds into my arms
And we know just where
We both want to be.

Yes I'm old, not too old,
And I'm not dead
I just loose my head
Each time I fall in love

And I want to fall in love.
And I want to love her
And I want to be hers
To love and share love.

I really don't want to be alone
I want to wake up in the morning
With my arms still around her
Not around my pillow.

To smell the scent of her hair
And feel the softness of her cheek
And the warmth of the covers
Causing us to snuggle closer.

To know that we are safe
In each other's arms
And the morning dawns
On this day together

I look at her next to me
And I forget all my pains
For I have suffered
Like all poets have

But I am softened
By her sweet smile
And her quiet voice
And her lingering kiss.

Hold me, My precious,
Find things to fill our time
With each others dreams
That we don't fear to whisper.

For we whisper together
And conspire together
As people in love have done
Since Eve ate that apple.

It wasn't wrong then
And it's not wrong now,
And nothing feels so right
As you in my arms.

So stay here forever,
Where we belong.
Let the world spin around
And let the seasons change

For time has no meaning
For those in love
For only in love
Is there meaning for lovers.

I hear the other poets whine
About one night stands
And waking up afterwards
Alone and without love

And it reminds me why
I want to keep this love
To wake up into every morning
With beauty in my arms.

Yes, I want love to last.
I still believe in love
And I believe in you
And that feels great.

08/28/2002

Story on Summer Kids

Have you ever had to spend time at the airport during summer vacation?

Did you get to observe the summer ritual of child shipping that appears ubiquitous around the boarding gates?

I, like other divorced fathers, am court ordered to ship my children back to a former spouse. I witnessed other heartrending scenes like mine all around me while I shipped my children off to that woman that betrayed me.

And as I looked at these scenes I saw men wiping tears from their eyes. Failing in their attempts to act like the heartless men their ex-wives tell their friends they are. And also the children crying openly because they must leave one they love for another they love.

I learned this year to run late to the airport. This puts the emotion and effort into getting to the plane on time and leaves you no time for the cranial rumination that causes the tears at that gate. That way you don't have to join those red eyed dads at the gate. You can wait till you get back to your car and cry in private like a real man.

Yes, I cry after I ship off my kids to their mom. But I wait till I get home to that empty house and clean up after the mad rush to get them off on time. As a police officer I have learned to be professional at the scene. You can puke later when you won't mess up the scene rather than leaving the contents of your stomach to obscure vital evidence. Other fathers are not as cool as I am, they are not trained to be cool. Or again maybe I am that heartless man she says I am.

08-14-2001

STREAMS OF THE HEART

If our love was something tangible,
      Nothing made by the puny hands of man
            Could contain it

Its volume is unimaginable,
      It is more than we fathomed
            It could be years ago

Our love continues to flower
      As if it could cover the world
            Bit by little bit.

And we can feel this hour
      Both the depth and the breadth
            That it can grow.

Yesterday I held you in my arms
      At our own holy ground above
            A babbling and whispering brook.

Then we waded in its waters
      Cooling our feet on the rocks
            Throwing back the years.

The years have been good,
      No harms have failed to pull us together.
            We've nourished our dreams.

As a pair of playful otters
      We've raised our family
            In streams of happy tears.

SUMMER KIDS

XX's & OO's for my X & Y's

My house will be quiet tomorrow
After a month of steady noise.
My kids go back to their mother
And I'll pack away their toys.

I'll be alone again for eleven months.
My power bill will lower.
The only noise coming from my yard
Will be the power mower.

It has its plus and minuses
To spend so long alone.
It's not like I'm a hermit
I've the Internet and phone.

But three bedrooms are empty,
The nintendo sits unplugged,
The computer gets a rest from games,
And there's no food on the rug.

I won't be running all the time
Hauling kids from here to there.
I won't be spending wads of cash
For things to manage hair.

But I'll miss the hugs and kisses
For all the rest the year
Until they come again next summer
With suitcase, trunk, and gear.

08-06-2001

Taste of Steel

So many times, over so many years
                    You were dispatched to calls like this.
Some who had completed the deed,
                    Some only tried and shied and missed.
And now your mouth tastes of steel
                    With a touch of Hoppes Number Nine
And you question if it's worth it
                    To tread that thin blue line.
Do the pressures of life press again
                    To make you question life's worth?
Do you tire of fighting a battle
                    As a clod against the roaring surf?
Has your wife left your home again
                    Because she can't understand your drive
That makes you pin on that badge
                    And strap a pistol on your side?
Do only other cops understand you?
                    Can only other cops feel this way?
Has that shield made you so different
                    That you want to leave this way?
Do you feel that your effort's wasted
                    On people who will never realize
That you've sworn you will protect them
                    and their homes, their shops, their lives?
Do you feel that its a service
                    When you stop a speeding car?
After all, it wasn't really dangerous
                    And they weren't going very far.
Then you have to pull a child
                    A twisted body from a car
To be covered with a blanket
                    When it's resting on the tar.
No one stops to say thank you
                    For the horrid job you've done
And they never face the family
                    When you tell them they've no son.
Maybe sucking steel is a privilege
                    For a cop who has reached the wall
And he makes his last reflections
                    As the hammer swiftly makes its fall.

TEARS FOR TIMMY

For Tim Linden

We reach out and ... our hands come back empty
    No longer can we grasp your hand, old friend
For we've chosen to go further along the road
    And you have chosen oblivion, bringing your own end.

It is not our place to judge your action.
    For you have fled beyond the bounds of mortality
Into the realms we accept only by our faith
    Where the mystery is known and becomes your reality.

It saddens us, your friends, that you have gone
    Away from us at this time and in this way.
For we wonder if we, by other words unsaid,
    Could have changed this fate and prevented this day.

We come at last together to bid you goodbye
    But feel cheated and empty for you're not here.
It is like waving adieu to a fleeing shadow.
    We can not hear you or hold you near

So this is what's left ... We and our memories.
    We have loved the time we have spent with you.
We have shared your humor and heard your stories.
    With tears we say goodbye. We'll miss you, Adieu.

11-10-96

The Day that turned to Hell

Have you ever had one of those horrid assignments in school that confirms your belief that your teacher is a truly sick quasi-human splash of protoplasm?

Here I am sitting across from an old, bald, half-blind, decaying fossil that is supposed to tell me what it was like in the riots at the millennium. This bulbous lump is lucky if he can remember his name. And he was a sworn officer that actually survived the mobs in the old west. Just like in the movies. He's squinting at me now through his one good eye framed by glasses that are so thick the weight seems to crush his nose. My recorder is running as I wait for him to get his thoughts together. You can almost hear the old neurons creaking into action in that wrinkled old dome of a head.

"Well kid, I guess that teacher of yours wants me to give you a history lesson."
rattles from the ancient lump across the table.

"Yes, sir," I answer shifting in my seat amazed I can even understand him.

"You've probably seen all about it on the old video clips. You've seen them haven't you." he grumbles

I answer, "Yes, But we are supposed to learn what it was actually like to live through a piece of history. Kind of an eye witness."

"You know," He says, "A lot of people who didn't live through the mobs were friends of mine. You see the old news videos and you forget that each of those people had names and families, Parents and lovers. All they were trying to do was to survive till the next day in a day that turned to hell.

"One of the things they make you do when you pinned on a badge in those days was to swear an oath. An oath to protect the constitution against all enemies, Domestic of foreign. You never thought you'd be looking down your sights at neighbors whipped into a panic by fear, by hunger, by thirst, and by the media. When the lights went out in the cities the skies were soon lighted by the flames of society hitting the wall.

"At first nuts were shooting their guns into the midnight sky to celebrate the change of the year. but when the power went out and the water pressure dropped things went wild."

The old guy shifted in his chair and seemed to reflect on the events of thirty years ago. Then he let out a sigh and continued. "I was working day watch at the Jail in Reno. I was smart enough to stay at home that night. I usually went dancing on New Years Eves. But we were on call for the next days even on our regular days off. We were assigned to work through our weekend. We had prepared.

"Doomsayers were predicting that people would panic when the lights went out. But we all had been in the dark before. We all had lanterns and candles. It was later when the water quit flowing that things got intense. Thirst was something none of them had been counting on. Few of them had water. Within a day thirst drove them into a frenzy.

"It took the power companies just days to get things up and running again. But a couple days without water killed a couple million in the riots.

We learned that if our snipers took out the leaders things would quiet down for a while. Fires couldn't be put out without water. That meant anyone with a firebomb or a torch had to be shot on sight. It was hard to shoot people you lived near. People you saw at the store or the gas pumps. But to save your city or town you did what had to be done.

"It's a terrible sight to see a bunch of people coming down the street at you. I had faced riots before. Sixty years ago when the Viet Nam War was going both protests and riots were common. But these weren't activists or protesters. These were neighbors without water. logic and planning was on our side not theirs. I had 20 gallons of water at my house. That was worth a fortune.

"You try to forget the faces you saw in your cross hairs that exploded."

At that she uttered, "I don't understand sir."

"You can't kid." He said quietly, "Unless you lived through it you can't understand what it was like. Maybe that's why they call it history. you know -- his, the pronoun and story, a tale from the past.'

I reached down and turned the recorder off and sat back. Man, People actually lived through stuff like that in history!

12-13-99

The Amazing Mumford

It was just another spring evening in Reno. I parked my car in the reserved parking space next to the Reno Justice Court Building. I use that because it is posted so only a member of the Sheriff's Office can park there without being ticketed. If I place my card on my dash board I can use the space and not have to go looking for a place to park.

I walked over to the pedestrian bridge across to Wingfield Park and walked across the park to the other bridge. This took me to the amphitheater that is between the Java Jungle and the Riverside theater. I was there to read poetry with some other poets that meet every Monday just to read.

I was talking to some of the regulars and an intoxicated street person staggered up to panhandle. I looked at him and said, "The Amazing Mumford, How are you doing?"

He looked at me and in his alcohol clouded mind tried to remember who called him that. His name was really Medford but I had began calling him Mumford because he reminded me of the inept magician from Sesame Street. He bore a strange resemblance to the Muppet and his intoxicated antics did not belay the similarity.

To my surprise he took offense to the remark instead of remembering it was the old deputy at the jail that always called him that.

He said in a thick tongued voice, "I don't like to be called that." And proceeded to pull off his black leather jacket. This took longer than he anticipated in his alcohol induced state and looked a lot less threatening than he was trying to act. He took a step toward me and threw his jacket on the ground.

The act drew the attention of a few of the poets and they stopped their conversations to see what the trouble was. I started talking with Medford in a quiet voice and tried to remind him where he knew me from. It started to sink into his booze softened skull that I was a cop and therefore armed and fairly good in a fight.

I changed to my command voice and told him to pick up his jacket. He looked at the jacket then back at me. I told him again more firmly to pick up the jacket. He again looked at the jacket. I then told him in the form of an order to pick up his jacket. He reached down and grabbed it.

I reached in my pocket and handed him a five dollar bill. I told him he should get something in his stomach other than booze before he got himself into trouble. He said he was going to get a hit of Heroin and that would relax him. I figured that as long as I didn't have to kick some sense into him it would be O.K.

He staggered off to a guy dealing drugs on the river bank.

Later he came back to the amphitheater and he was my best friend. "I love ya, guy" and hugged me and slapped me on the back. Then he continued doing so until it became quite obnoxious. I would now have to delouse the clothing I was wearing as soon as I got home. I didn't need pets in my house. Flea bites are a real problem because I'm allergic to them and I get bumps an inch across when feasted upon. He finally waded across the river to a small island, I figure he was camping there in sight of the court house. Most cops don't like to wade in a uniform and dress shoes to see where the drunks pass out.

The next morning I heard he was back in the jail sobering up for a while. When he was sentenced and again in the housing unit I was working I reminded him of the incident and he had no recollection at all. I suppose that's all right because he won't remember where I am Monday nights to bum more money from me.

Such is life.

08/31/01

The Apple Hill Event

Sure, I'd been there before. I knew the streets and the general lay of the land. What I didn't know was the location of the Bank of America.

Here we were a hundred miles from home. We had come to Placerville to visit Apple Hill. Everyone around here knows the fruit stands and craft booths that are scattered along the roads between the fruit groves. We had driven all those miles to be here. We had even got up early and left Reno before the air race traffic made it hard to navigate.

We had planned to stop at a B of A along the way and pull a couple hundred out of the Versateller. I will not use the tellers of another bank because I am very stubborn about paying those costly foreign bank charges. I feel that it's throwing my money away. I would rather spend it on garbage and sparklies at the booths along the road ahead.

I had remembered seeing the B of A on a previous trip through the area but I couldn't remember upon which road it was located.

I told my girlfriend that we would just cruise the main street and stop at the bank because I thought it was there. We were cruising east on highway 50 from Sacramento where we had taken the exit just before highway 49. I followed the main street parallel to highway 50 and looked carefully for the bank. I knew the bank was there. All I needed was a couple hundred of mad money for the day.

We weaved our way until the road curved right at the outskirts of Placerville and we came to the end. we took a right reasoning it would take us back to town. We kept following the "logical" roads. We found the road to the hospital. Maybe the bank was near there. The road dead-ends at the hospital on the of a hill. So we turn around and head back down the hill. I take a left and follow the road around the hill. Yep, the road ends right there. Look up, There's the hospital. Turn around again.

It's down the hill and then we're at a Hospital sign again. We turn the other way. and find ourselves at the road we first got on from Highway 50. Then once more we go through town. We're approaching Highway 49 again. I'm getting tired of looking. I'm going to have to stop and ask directions. We turn left and up a road. a kind of a triangle to Highway 49 southbound. There's a fire station and my girlfriend suggests we stop and ask directions.

Now as a real man it is against the "oath of testosterone" to ask directions. But in the cause of saving our relationship I will condescend and ask directions. But I'm already past the point where we can safely pull into the driveway of the firestation. The firemen are in front. We drive by and I tell her we will go around the triangular block and ask them directions.

I pull into the driveway just past the station and realize we're sitting turning in the parking lot of the Bank of America, Placerville branch. My girlfriend starts giggling. It advances to a real laugh. I begin to see her point and I stop at the teller machine and we tease each other.

Can you imagine violating the "Oath of testosterone" and pulling into a firestation to ask directions with the destination right next door. I would have had to turn in my macho permit. I would have been embarrassed so badly I could never have shown my face again at a football game. I would have been forced to watch Monday night football alone, forever alone.

I basked in the silence as I withdrew ten twenties from the machine. I blew a healthy amount of that cash as hush money paid to my girlfriend. Now she will never be able to tell the story of my breaking the taboo and almost having to ask directions.

Oh, The shame of it all.

09/25/2000

THE CREEK

If you ignore the noise
      Of the cars going by
You can hear the water
      Of the nearby creek
As it falls across the rocks
      And heaves its sigh
It brings solace to your soul
      And makes you weak.

Weak may not be the word,
      Maybe it is soft,
Halcyon moments stolen in a world
      Of the hard,
The beam set to balance
      The scales across;
Leveling the stress of life
      As a playing board.

You can feel the blood pressure
      Lower and slow.
The pace of the day
      Can melt away
As you listen to the water
      Make its hurried flow
As it passes over the rocks
      On its way.

11-10-95

THE CYCLE OF A BIRD SONG

It's the longest day of the year
    and I woke to the singing of a bird.
It doesn't matter to him that my alarm
    Won't go off for another hour or so.
He only knows that it is light enough
    For him to read the notes of his score.
He sings the song of the birds of his kind
    Hoping his voice will reach the tender ears
Of one that will fall to his charm
    And share his nest and bare his eggs
Following the way of the singing birds
    Since wings carried them off to the valley floor.
The yearly cycle of egg to bird to egg
    Each male learning the single song of love
That touches the heart bringing her blood warm.
    Leading her to the top of my cedar fence
Where he waits and sings his morning song
    That will win her heart forever more.

6/26/2009

THE COMET

We search with care the heavens
And pick among the stars
Searching for the stranger there
Visiting space we call Ours.

But it has been here before
And for eons has ignored
The growth of men upon this world,
Just specks upon this orb.

Whole lives are just a blink to it
As it falls toward the Sun.
It doesn't care we waste our days
Shuffling paper by the ton.

We fear that he will come too close,
To smack us on the head.
For in a flash of fire and steam
We'd turn from quick to dead.

A point of light with a trailing tail
That fades across the sky.
A smudge, a streak, a smear, a blot,
It tries to fool the eye.

Scientists seek to plot it a course
And lovers on it dream.
A hunk of rock, of ice, of gas,
Bright tail a puff of steam.

03-18-97

THE DAY TO REST

The sun is shining on the green hill;
The ground is damp from the mornings rain;
The sky is blue with spots of white;
But it's beautiful all the same.

My heart is full with joy and life;
On this day which we have to rest;
I know it's not long but it's needed;
And sufficient if used to our best.

1970

THE FALLEN KNIGHT

TO FRANK MINNIE

A knight has fallen from his mount
His helm and armor were as naught
His sworn companions could not help
Nor leech nor doctor they had sought.

Three days of vigil did we keep
Until his body breathed its last
And left us with but to mourn
Into our memories we let him pass.

We feel the loss of a brother boon.
Many a tale we've shared long passed.
And foes we've taken to their cells
To pay their debts of fortune cast.

Long has he fought the noble fight
And to his knighted oath was true.
He wore his shield on armored chest
His duty, charge, and goal he knew.

He answered to the beck and call,
Day or night he did not shirk
To do his part, his shoulders tall,
Proud to do this toilsome work.

Well Done, Well fought, our noble friend
Many tales we still shall tell.
But this at last we say of you
The spurs of knighthood fit him well.

06-02-97

THE "FIRST TIME" PROMPT

It must have been the first time,
But it was so long ago it seems
Like I was always meant to rhyme,
To find that word to shape a dream.
I see pictures made of flowery words
That paint with brushes in your mind
That forms an image at times obscured
If that's the way your taste inclined.
Picking words out one by precious one
To draw the reader through my eyes
To see a moment that's taken from
The lay of the land … How it lies.
Or picture a person, a shape of a face,
A curve of a body that I describe,
The shade of the skin that hints of race
The ripple of muscle, an eye that cried,
The flow of a river, a rush of wind,
The sound of the traffic rushing past,
The birds singing spring from yonder limb,
The whine of a puppy, the rustle of grass.

04/06/2012

The Flash of Light

The flash of light/ the roar of thunder/ the
smell of the wet sagebrush/ then the odors of
smoke/ and burning desert/ and flames coming on
in a rush./ The cheat grass and wind/ encourage
the speed/ as the fire works toward us./ and
the thin band of red/ paints black the desert
like a brush./
Hotshots and brush rigs/ roll into action
pumping water/ and cutting fire lines/ knocking
down the flames,/ narrowing the front,/
protecting the homes and the pines,/ while
those of us down wind/ fill cars and SUV's with
treasures of other times/ and plan to run
before the flames/ with what we can.

06-26-2002

THE MILITARY ATTITUDE

My life is as a leaf
Blown in the wind aimlessly
As this time blows forth
In a way I cannot control.
Forced to accept things without question,
Very little can I change.
I want to guide it now
But it moves on constantly
Driven from place to place and
From role to other roles
And I feel there's naught to do
As far as I can arrange,
But I shant give up hope in
Seeking new direction and new definity
That I can find and follow
My own pathway to eternity.

1971

THE PEN

The pen of a poet
   Puts no salt on his table
But is flavor and spice
   In the soul of his reader.
His worth is measured
   Not in who remembers him
But who remembers the words
   Scribed upon some lines
He scratched years ago
   In hours before dawn
While others were asleep
   Or doing the things
That don't really matter
   In the light of day.

12/24/2003

05-08-00

The Poacher

There he is down below me. I can see the orange spot of his hunter's hat as he moves in and out of the shadows. I can't see his rifle but it looks like he has a large handgun in a shoulder holster. He sure moves in and out of the shadows smoothly. This hunter really seems to know how to hunt.
He hunts silently.
If it wasn't for that orange hat I couldn't locate him at all.
He stops in an open patch and kneels to examine a track. I get the spotting scope on him before he moves out. I don't see a hunting license on his hat or chest. I think I can hook me a poacher this time.
There he's moving again. He's overweight but in good shape. But he moves slowly. He must be near his prey.
Look at that guy. He moves and freezes. He stays, then he moves in and out of the shadows, behind a tree, then to a brush, then to a rock. He looks to be stepping on rocks when he can. I bet he's making as little noise as possible. It's just like watching a dance. He pauses like the pauses between the lines of a tango, before you step out after the step, side draw.
He's frozen now. It's minutes before he moves slowly up the hill. He checks for tracks. He moves in a croach across a small patch of grass heading for some rocks.
There.... Can you see the doe? She's in a group of boulders. One slants down and back in and shelters her from the sun and wind. She could lay there and hide from anything. Anything except this relentless hunter. He's going to poach this doe. But I'll have him in jail by nightfall. I've blocked in his truck and put the CLUB across his steering wheel.
He's a couple of hundred feet from the doe now. He's moving in from the down wind side like a coyote. He's really slow now. He moves a few yards and stops as he chooses a path that will cause less noise. He moves again, slowly.
Can you see how he moves. Every time she looks his way he freezes like a rock. She's color blind like all deer. She can't see his orange hat. But she could see movement if he wasn't doing the walk and freeze of a stalker. This hunter's a pro.

He's fifty feet from her now. This guy knows his stuff. Most hunters take a hundred yard shot or have one chased across his line of fire to get a deer. But this guy is going to get close enough to take the doe with that handgun. He's already within range.
But he's not taking his gun out. He's moving closer. I steady my spotting scope on its tripod to get a good look at him. I wish I had a camera hooked up to it. This would get me a trophy. This guy is art work.
He freezes for a long time, three minutes, four. How does he do it? That doe looks right at him and he just pretends he's not there. Then she looks away and he moves closer, then a few feet to the left and behind a rock to rest. Leaning there he rests in the shade just thirty feet from her and she doesn't have a clue that death lurks there. There, he moves again, closer and closer, like a lion in those nature films just before he springs and crushes his prey. Its going to be a shame to put cuffs on this guy.
He rounds a rock. He's now ten feet from the doe. She swings her head around and looks right into his eyes. He doesn't even twitch. She has no fear of him. She must see him now. She looks away and he inches even closer. He could club her with that gun now but it still rests in the holster.
Hold it.
He's backing off. He doesn't shoot the doe. She still is undisturbed in the rocks as he backs away. He's stalking backwards as easily as he had forward. He backs away taking his time. He moves more quickly as the distance increases. That big doe doesn't know how close she's come to being gutted and hung to cool by the stalker. He moves out of her sight and around the edge of the hill. He moves out at a fast rate. He begins to whistle a tune that carries across the valley to me. I see the doe's ears perk up but she can tell the sound is moving away so it bodes her no danger. She lays down in the shade.
The hunter crosses the valley and heads toward the trucks. I stay hidden. He switches back and forth up the mountain. Sometimes he heads my way, then cuts back across away from me. He's a hundred meters off and heading back this way. He stops and plops his butt down on a rock.
He scans below and above. He looks left and right. He rests about five minutes. He rises and stretches. He flexes,

chasing away the exertion and he starts up the hill again, coming closer with each step.

"You still up there warden?" His voice carries up to me. It's the first sound he's made in two hours. I feel violated. He knew I was up here all along.

I rise up to his view and answer, "Ya, Right here."

He eyes me and I eye the big autoloader at his left shoulder. It's in a quick draw cop rig. The grips are covered with rubber PACHMAYR grips. They show wear like a duty weapon.

"I hope I was entertaining enough not to waste all your time on me today." He states in a "matter of fact" way. I sense he's a cop.

"You didn't take that doe down there." I observe.

He responds, "No, I never intended to kill her. She wasn't doing anything but looking like a beautiful doe."

"That's a lot of work to come away empty handed."

"But the sports in being able to do it. Like the plains Indian scoring a coup by touching an opponent without getting hurt. At home my prey shoots back. Shooting a defenseless doe isn't quite sporting to me."

"I thought I pegged you for a cop." I said.

"And good enough to stay alive all these years." and together we head back for the trucks.

The Quail

The fat Quail sits on the top Strand
Overlooking his covey of beauties
As they forage safely below him
Among the grasses and leaves.
There, in the warm spring sun,
Feeds the future of his little domain,
Pecking seeds from the dry earth
As some clouds mount, Promising rain.
And I drive by, Hardly noticed,
On the hard black roadway
Not a threat to the many birds
As they eat their days away.
Kevin Lieby

ON THE WINGS OF A DREAM

On the wings of a dream
Life slowly unfolds
Like an emergent butterfly
Flexing in color
And drying in the sun
To a rigid sheet
That will soar and ply
The blue skies
On its short lived run.
And I still tremble at life
And all it holds,
And all its hidden mysteries
Around each bend
As the days and years come
As the earth turns
And the minute our hour flees
Except the ones we seize
As they make their headlong run.
Grab a minute here or there
And scribe it
In a verse or a line.
Make it forever,
Done and yet undone,
Frozen as it were,
That short moment of time
Etched on a line,
Captured, as it tried to run

5/22/2002

THE SPANISH SWORD

My steel is bright and sure
Molten from Spanish Ore
Rolled out into steel plate
Being flawless to the core.

Crude strips formed into blade
My tip and tang shaped to form
Sharpened edge cut to the fore
With pommel is proudly borne.

Grip wrapped with twisted wire
Made soft with fire and heat
Guard hammered, twisted, forged
Where art and battle meet.

Made in the martial cause
To frighten and rout the moor
Wielded by a Spanish hand
In the days of yore.

Hanging now upon the wall
In honor with pommel high
I can come to use again
When called by hue and cry.

06-05-00

THE RETIREMENT

For Chuck Stoffel

More than one cried … when he put up his guns
And laid down that badge made of tin.
For twenty odd years, he had worn them with pride
And our streets were more safe 'cause of him.

We'd walked long together under storm cloud and sun
But we knew we weren't out there alone.
But it's time, my old buddy, to hang up your guns
And pick up your bags and go home.

Every day we were there with workin' to do.
More than once you were there at my side
When the shit hit the fan, or a fugitive ran,
And you weren't just along for the ride.

Retirement's here and the winters are cold
It's not fun anymore on the street.
It's hard to imagine that we're getting old
And this duty gets hard on the feet.

More time will you have for your little white balls,
May they never fall far from the cup,
May your fairways be smooth, and your greens ever small,
And your eyes, ever keen, when you putt.

May your old alarm ring, Many hours after mine,
May you not have to get up at all.
May your memories mellow with time just as wine
And when you have one, Please give me a call.

01-22-2001

THE ROAD

The road winds along a stream
Flashing both blue and silver
Filling a valley with green
Splashed with blossoms of ever color.

Open windows gently cool the car
And brings us the sweet scents
Of each flower near and far
Which makes this time intense.

The sun dashes back and forth
Along the crest of the canyon.
Sun and shade, Sun and shade,
As if drawn by a crayon.

And we talk gentle words of life
Kind of leaving our minds in neutral
As we cruise we kind of describe
What we're seeing as we travel.

Squirrels and rabbits scamper away
To hide in the sheltering grasses
And thus they live another day
Peeking as our car passes.

We share a moment with these
And pass on down the stream
Disturbing not even the trees
Cruising as if in a dream.

06-18-99

THE SMILE YOU'VE GIVEN ME

Our eyes meet from across the room
And your smile invites me to your table.
We have met and spoken before
But now both spark, and touch enable.
We seem to reach out to each other.
We enjoy the verse from the little stage.
The writings of our group of poets
Merged with the poems stolen from another age.
And we banter and give accolade
To the brave souls grasping the mic
Who from memory or from rumpled paper
Emote, these poems in the night.
It gives me time to hold your hand
And run my fingers in your hair
And you could do the same to mine
If there was anything growing up there.
Our short time together is but a promise
Of maybe ... some future times to come.
But now I barely know your name,
Where you're going, or where you're from.
But the moments here excite me,
They leave me wanting more and more.
And I wonder if you'll come again
Will you grace again our door.
And share the poems of your soul
And give us time to understand
What is hidden deep inside you
Be it petty, Be it grand.
Come again and join our number
Better yet come join with me
And we'll see just what develops
From that smile you've given me.

01/31/2002

THE TUNNEL'S END

There is a light at the end of this tunnel.
Those rumors were true all these years
But the struggle was long to just get here.
It felt that sometimes we just stuck in the gears.

Nothing was easy, it was just like they said.
The Tunnel was dark and it went on so long
Sometimes we struggled but sometimes we flew.
There were detours. we wondered where we had gone.

But now nears the end of our journey.
The way to the exit lies open and clear.
Behind us are trials and piles of memories.
Left behind as yesterdays baggage, cobwebs obscuring the years.

We'll finally have some time just for fishing.
The alarm clock will be found in the trash.
We'll have what we want when we want it,
If we can only come up with the cash.

The grandkids will arrive just like locust
And wipe out our food in the fridge.
Their parents will drop them off often
So we can sugar them up just a smidge.

We'll tell them of life in the old days
Those days and nights working the beat,
From the ease of our well worn recliners,
'cause we're taking a load off our feet.

y 2007

The way of the Blossom

It was a promise.
It was a hope.
It was a vision
Of joy to come.

But as the blossoming
Of the apple tree,
As it sends forth
It's bloom each spring,

Just to be bitten
By the spring frosts,
Then petals fall away
Dried by the sun.

So was your promise
Early in its season
Casting your fruit early
Not by your causing.

The promise was there.
The joy of hope.
You felt now lost,
Disappointed, standing bare

As is my tree.
Full of colorful leaves
And promise of strength
But limbs not ladened

But it goes on
All summer long
Spreading forth in leaf
And sweetening the air.

In its yearly cycle,
Hoping next years frost
Will miss its buds,
Its fruit to ripen.

It does not wither
From one years loss
But knows the seasons
That come each year.

Some year its fruit
Will hang its boughs
Low and heavy hung
With fruit so sweet

That memories of years
When it didn't bare
Are like yesterday's fog
That's no longer here.

The cycle goes on
Days pass into years
The leaves go yellow
Then the rhythms repeat.

07/08/97

THE WHISTLER

The whistling comes from out in the desert
      It trills out loudly not bashful or subdued
So we know the whistler is out there alone.
      Whistling can be a key to his attitude.

The whistler shares his tunes with the coyotes
      And the animals that scurry out of his way.
He shares music with the moon and the stars.
      Sharing with them the victories of the day.

In his carefree melodies he knows he's alone.
      No fear of criticism or complaint holds him back
But he musically frolics to please only himself.
      Not knowing or fearing what's out in the black.

Freedom is what he feels because no one cares
      That he is enjoying his music in the mountains
With none to please but himself and the rocks
      And critters that wonder in their holes
            what the commotion is.

09-12-99

THEY COME

They come.
They come.
Night after night
Rank after rank
Row upon row
Like a Kansas cornfield
Like a progression of waves,
Pounding upon the beach
And grinding the stones
Into grains of sand.

They come.
They come.
We see them.
We hear them.
Day upon day
The drone of their voices
Bring us the words
We don’t want to hear
Irritating, Like a small pebble
Moving about in your shoe.

They come.
They come.
Again and again
Frame after frame
Over and over
Repeating and replaying
Showing us what we’ve seen
Burning it into our brains
Hammering again and again

At our open and bleeding wounds.
They come.
They come.
Cast by cast
Byte by byte
Channel upon channel
Their talking heads yapping
And spinning out the tales
Dragging out the hours and days
Preempting any chance of peace
Or sidestep into reality.

They come.
They come.
Horde of hordes
Camera after camera
Mic after mic
Telling us how to feel.
Telling us how they feel.
Telling and telling until we
Feel like they feel like we feel.

They come.
They come.
Newscast by newscast
Reporter by reporter
Hammering our opinion into
Their opinion into truth.
Surely it's the truth.
Maybe it's the truth.
We're told it's the truth.
So help me Dan Rather.

10/28/2001

THIS MOON, THIS NIGHT

A billion people will see this moon tonight.
So why do we call it ours?
Is it because we share this time,
And wish upon the stars?
Do its beams seem stronger
When reflected off the waves
Of the crystal waters of Tahoe,
Like tile with silver inlays?
Or are those moonbeams stronger
'Cause perchance we are near
The source of their powers and
The sky is so clear?
Or do these feelings come
Because you are close?
Just because it's our perfect night
And we're wearing fancy clothes?
We hear the water brush by
Pushed by the wheel
But no waves can be found
To be cut by our keel.
The surrounding mountain crests
Close about our sides
As we enter the bay
Where the stone castle resides.
And the boat makes a slow turn
Around the small isle,
A gem in the Emerald Bay.
You can feel its ghost smile.
Now it's down to the dancing,
Swaying to the band,
On the crowded dancing floor
Speakers near at hand.
We finish up on the beach
Looking back at the lake
Where we lived another dream
For our memories sake.
10-10-2000

The Tower War

With simile and metaphor
      We write some lines
We crash and bore
      In stanzas and in rhymes.

We think we're great
      We can write sublime
Though we hardly rate
      'Cause we waste our time

Writing poems of love
      Though the towers fall
And we praise the dove
      And we shop the mall.

Do we think to help
      Or just jack our jaws
As our candles melt
      And life gives us pause?

What do we really do
      Or what have we done
While others fight for you
      And labor in the sun.

Our freedoms have a cost,
      A heavy and horrid price,
Many a life is lost
      And the work isn't nice.

All you can think of
      Is you don't want to go.
Carry a sign, chant, "love"
      "Hell no, we won't go"

If terror has its way
      We'll be hiding in caves
And men living this day
      Will go down to their graves.

It's a war we don't want.
      One that we didn't start.

Because of evil men's rant
    They struck at our heart.

We must capture the vermin
    Keep dogs on their track
'Cause creeps like Ben Laden
    Will always come back.

And any that hide him
    Must crumble and burn.
To wine him and dine him
    Gets your ash in an urn.

We've given him warning
    And we've tried to play fair
While a bull's-eye we're painting
    On that rag on his hair.

We know that he's hiding
    In a cave like a bat
With him and his henchmen
    Forced to sleep on a mat.

He has to be knowing
    That whenever he's found
This nation will place him
    Six feet in the ground.

It'll be Osama Ben Laden
    With the title "The Late"
When you screw with an American
    You've cast your own fate.

10-01-2001

THORA'S BIRTHDAY

There once was a little red headed girl
Just as smart as she was pretty
She moved away to her daddy's grief
Now she's grown up and turning thirty.

It doesn't seem to be right
And it isn't very fair
That she's having that party
Way the heck over there.

And he just wants to share
His wishes for her on her birthday
'cause her old dad still misses her
And she's just so far away.

But happy birthday, you precious girl,
Give my hugs to all those little ones.
Remember I love you with all of my heart
With kisses and hugs by the tons.

Dad (Kevin Lieby)

To loose a son

I heard, I heard,
The grief, the grief,
        To loose a son,
I can't understand,
And neither could he,
        What he has done.

The loss, the loss,
The pain, the pain,
        A son is gone.
The parting was swift
Nor were there signs
        That something was wrong.

The guilt, the guilt,
If I, If I,
        Could I have known?
Could I have done
But a bit more
        Here in the home?

The doubt, the doubt,
We wonder, we wonder,
        He was a bud,
Just a blossoming man
With flower just showing
        Reaching from the mud.

Not him, not him,
Not mine, not mine,
        It's just not right
That he is gone
No more to dream
        No more to fight.

Come back, come back,
Don't go, don't go.
        But choice is gone.
Choice made in haste
That is now over.
        He touched the pawn.

But now, but now,
We hurt. We hurt.
        The loss we feel
The pain is ours
For we have sons
        With whom we deal.

We cry, we cry,
We pray. We pray
        That ours may choose
To live and stay
A time with us,
        Come win or loose.

We reach, We reach
To you, To you
        Who bears the pain
That we do not.
But in our hearts
        The loss is plain.

Reach out. Reach out.
We're here. We're here
        Trying to stay near
And ease your pain,
Not quite knowing how
        To help our peer.

Our hearts, our hands,
Our prayers, our tears,
        Are ours to share
With one we know
From years of work
        And service and care.

Our friend, our brother,
Our peer, our fellow,
        We cry with you.
Your loss is ours.
And share your pain.
        We stand beside you.

2006

To My Fellow Poets At the Esoteric

Sometimes I wonder why.
            Why I come here every week.
I look at you burning
            With the hormones of youth
And me with my shoulders
            Aching with the pains of age.
I listen to your poetic tirades
            Against power and society.
Yet here I still carry a shield
            And allow you to be free.
You, of youth, are driven by
            Your wishes and your fantasies
And I am driven by my duties
            But I can share poems and memories.
I listen to your poems of
            One night stands and disappointments
And I smile, for I too have
            My regrets and scars and resentments
Do you think that at my age
            I can feel no more like you do?
That I no longer yearn
            For the ladies I would once pursue.
At my age I still know
            The thrill of the chase, I'm not dead.
And the hormones and passion,
            Though mellow, still run through my head...
Which turns to follow as you
            Lovely young ladies stroll by
And my pulse still quickens
            When I catch a flash of your thigh.
But I do not threaten you
            Like those boys of your own tender age
Who just want you for a quickie
            A single scene upon a page.

I look for a little more now
            Than just a roll across the mattress
Like evenings by the fireplace,
            The flickering lights, the warm caress,

Or spending hours together
Just spending time along the river
Talking of years to come,
Not just for now, but for forever.
I have children that are your age
And I do not yearn for more.
And I treat you as I do them
Like my children, Nothing more...
And I feel closer to you
Because we share the bond of poetry.
That glimpse into each others heart
That our verse alone sets free.
My children too are poets.
I have framed upon my wall
Poems that they have written.
They have heard the Muses' call.
Like their daddy has before them
They have found the joy of verse
And we share the gift together
Though it fattens not our purse.
And we find ourselves pursuing
Just some stanzas we can rhyme
And we share our poems together
there's no better use of time.
Do not look on me with pity
Just because I'm growing old and bald.
With time and luck maybe someday
You'll look like you've been mauled.
Don't treat me like and old fart,
Just treat me like a friend.
And let's share our poems together
We may even start a trend.

TOKEN

Speak we again of eternity
Held fast with a yellow gold band.
Know that I place it endearingly
On your finger that's held in my hand.

Take it, my love, as it's given
As a token that comes from my heart.
It shines as if it's come from heaven.
For it's there that love had its start.

A matching band fit on my finger.
I shall never forget what it's for.
For it, like memories, linger
To remind me it's you I adore.

Walk with me now down the aisle
That is lined on both sides with our friends.
Our love is cause of each smile.
"Best wishes" is the prayer each one sends.

It's off for a lifetime together.
It can go even farther for us.
It will stand against trials forever.
In a temple we sealed it thus.

03-05-2001

TRIALS

Why do things get in our way
      And take so long to figure out?
The things that test us every day.
      The things we always think about.
Is it a puzzle or a test
      To show us things we can do
To separate us from the rest
      That we can find ourselves anew?

REFLECTIONS OF TIME

There are times when things go easy.
      There are times when things go bad..
There are times when you are happy.
      There are times when you are sad.

I think these times are needful
      To make your life fulfilled
To keep your life from being dull
      So you can live until...

The time when you'll be always happy.
      When everything will go just right
For you'll return to your Maker someday
      And you'll dwell amid truth and light.

A TRIBUTE TO LARRY JOHNSON

WITH SHIELDS ENSHROUDED WE SALUTE A KNIGHT
THAT GAVE HIS ALL TO WIN THAT FIGHT
AND THUS LAYS COLD AND STILL THIS DAY
A FRIEND AND BROTHER HAS PASSED AWAY

TOO OFT WE HEED THE CALL TO ARM
AND PUT OURSELVES IN WAY OF HARM
TO KEEP THE PEACE AND UPHOLD THE RIGHT
TO MAKE A CITY'S STREETS SAFE AT NIGHT

BUT A VARLET'S RED HAND WITH A COWARDS BLOW
HATH STRUCK AND LAID HIS VALIANT HEART LOW
SO NOBLE AND BRAVE WAS HE THAT DAY
A FRIEND AND BROTHER HAS PASSED AWAY

WE ALL HAVE SWORN OURSELVES AS HE HAD
AND WORKED THE GOOD TIMES AND THE BAD
IN STORM AND SUNSHINE, IN LIGHT AND DARK
IN TIMES OF TRIAL WE'VE MADE OUR MARK

BUT NOW THAT MARK IS MADE ON US
AS TEARS DAMPEN OUR CHEEKS WE'RE TROUBLED THUS
BY THE MEMORIES ON THIS DAY IN MAY
A FRIEND AND BROTHER HAS PASSED AWAY

A LAST SALUTE AND HE IS LOWERED DOWN
MORE TEARS ARE SHED AND MANY'S THE FROWN
THAT CROSSES THE FACES AS WE PRAY
A FRIEND AND BROTHER HAS PASSED AWAY

5/23/95

TUNE

I'm so out of tune
Traveler must hate me.
But I don't have knobs
To tighten my steel strings.
I don't vibrate and twang
To bring music to man
But I use my words
To strike deep your soul.
You pick on me and
I'll break your fingers
But together we can
Strike that forgotten chord.
We could sync together gently
To hum and buzz melodic,
That song would ever sing
In our minds
To echo and reverberate in
The ears of others
Who may think we're out
of tune too.
Maybe it's just our strings
Are not wound up tight.
03-19-2012

TWENTY EIGHT LINES

This page has twenty eight lines
Etched and numbered down its side
Giving me the room to play a bit
With words that are, as yet, untried.
Do I write of the warm busy day
I have spent here in my cozy home
Or the time on a site on my computer
Or the time with a daughter on the phone.

I did take the time to finish an exciting book
About searching caves for things that shine
About spies and treasure and finding love
And breaking codes when running out of time.
Or do I tell you about my granddaughter
Singing out, "PaPa catch me!"
And running, giggling, through the house
As happy as she could possibly be.

Or watching with her "The Velveteen Rabbit"
When I could be working out in the yard.
But she's only three for one year
So that decision wasn't really so hard.
Then I find myself on the next page
Still writing about I was busy
But the needs of a sweet little granddaughter
Let my priorities get a bit fuzzy.

Show me a gramps with the time he needs
To squander his time brings her a smile
And I'll show you a man that, after all,
Knows that it only lasts this short while.
Give her the memories she will recall
When you stumble to think of her name.
She'll remember you chasing her all through the house
And how she started that game.
04/27/2009

Verse for John Bohach

Killed 08/22/2001

They say that shots rang out today
And took away a friend.
That left a gaping hole in life
It'll take us long to mend.
For it's never just a faceless name
That backs the badge of steel.
But one that we've stood shoulders with
When the pressures were getting real.
We take for granted blood will spill
At times along this road.
But we hope it's at a distance
While we're shouldering our load.
But now it's happened close again
It singes and it sears
For the name is not a faceless one,
Its mention brings forth tears.
One that we have called our friend
And often called our brother
Has passed beyond that final veil
And flowers are his cover.
Our minds will try to make some sense
Or meaning to his death.
But there never seem to be the words
To comfort the bereft.
It's but our lot to say goodbye
Until again we meet
We know your place will be with God
Your mansion at His feet.

Waves of life

I watch the waves lap the shore.
The tide is at climax right now.
I gaze and contemplate what they mean,
The why, the what, the when, the how.

Small waves, and yet they are so long.
The stretch as far as eye can see,
Churning the beach with its gentile lap.
The sounds of restless surf comes to me.

Our lives are waves so thin and long,
Yet joined together they form a mighty sea
That laps against the long shores of time;
Which moves the sands of memory.

Waves never end, nor do our lives end,
But move bending and curling toward our goal
That we may fulfill our purpose of life
That we may be each and eternal soul.

Yes; lives are waves and tempest tossed
Building higher and higher into the roaring surf.
And the years turn our tops white with age
As we venture onward from our hour of birth.

Will waves ever end? No this is true.
For they, as souls, will find no end
We shall look forward in haste
To eons of life just around the bend.

Yes; I think on, as I tarry here
And contemplate the meaning of the waves.
The end is obscured in the future.
Where it waits hidden far from our gaze.

"WAY OUT THERE"

EXT. ALKALI FLAT, HIGH NOON

Two men in business suits, shoes covered with dust, Tracks leading from them into the distance

RALPH - BLOTTING SWEAT FROM HIS FOREHEAD

Remind me - If we ever make it out of here - never to scam a guy whose name ends in a vowel. It seems to have gotten us into a lot of trouble.

JACK

Look at the bright side. If we were in New York we'd be looking at the fish going by and holding our breaths.

RALPH

I am looking at the bright side. Everything's bright out here. So it may take us a couple of days to become bird food instead of becoming instant fish food.

JACK

Didn't the doctor say you should get more sun and exercise every day?

RALPH

Somehow when he was saying I should firm up He wasn't suggesting a case of Rigor-Mortis, Smart-ass.

JACK

You were raised in the desert weren't you?
And weren't you in the Boy Scouts and in the Army?
You was trained to survive, weren't you.?
You wasn't raised in the city like me.

RALPH

I was raised in Reno. And in the middle of Reno is a river. There's a market on about every corner selling Big Gulps and that doesn't seem to add up to what we have here. Unless you can see some Pakistani polishing a counter up ahead.

THE CAMERA SHOWS THE MOUNTAINS RISING FROM THE DRY LAKE BED FAR IN THE DISTANCE.

Jack, If we make it all the way to that mountain before sunrise I think I can keep us alive for a while. Out here we're not going to be much except jerky much after sun up.

THE TWO START OFF TOWARD THE MOUNTAIN

INT. DARK BAR, ONLY A FEW PATRONS AND THEY'RE STAYING CLEAR OF TWO MEN IN SUITS SHARING A PITCHER OF BEER.

DUKE

How long do you think they're going to last out there, Johnny?

JOHNNY

About as long as this beer, Duke.
We damn near didn't make it back and we were in the car. Remind me to get that air conditioner fixed before we do that again.

DUKE

When are we going to tell the boss how we got rid of those two turkeys.

JOHNNY

I'm in no hurry. This beer isn't going to finish

itself.

INT - OFFICE OF SCARLOTTI up a dark stairwell from the bar, Scarlotti is on the phone.

SCARLOTTI

Yes sir. I put my best men on that assignment. If they ever find those two out in that dry lake there won't be enough left to identify.

Pause - unheard response on the line

SCARLOTTI

Yes sir, This way there's no bullets to trace, no fingerprints, no suspects, no evidence.

Short pause

SCARLOTTI

Yes sir, There's no way they can make it out. They're probably drinking mirage right now.

Scarlotti hangs up the phone. Pushes the intercom button.

SCARLOTTI

Paul, Are those two schmucks still at your bar?

VOICE OF PAUL

Yes sir, Just finishing the pitcher.

SCARLOTTI

Tell them to wash the car and be up here in half an hour.

VOICE OF PAUL

Yes sir.

EXT - ALKALI FLAT - two figures noticeably nearer the mountains - the sun is casting long shadows toward the mountains.

JACK

That breeze almost makes this heat bearable.

RALPH

You're going to be glad you kept the jacket like I told you about an hour ago.

JACK

Well, I didn't think we would make it this far. You sure kept me going when I wanted to set down.

RALPH

By the time it's dark we'll be in the foothills. See the light green patch there against the darker green hills. That's broad leaf plants among the darker juniper and sage. That's a water marker for us. The water's so shallow there you can dig for it with your hands. Which is fortunate because that is all we have.

JACK

I could drink mud right now. I feel weak and dry as a bone.

RALPH

If you'd have sat down back there you would be a bone by noon tomorrow. And we will drink mud. But we will be alive.

JACK

I knew you could save us

RALPH

We aren't saved by a long shot. Just a little better off than a corpse. If we can find that patch of light green when the moon is up we can have some water by morning. If we don't freeze tonight.

JACK

Freeze in the desert?

RALPH

Yes, freeze in the desert. There's no moisture in the air to hold the heat. That coat you have will be all that keeps you alive tonight.

JACK

Where'd you learn all this survival stuff?

RALPH

I read things other than the sports pages and Playboys. Maybe if I'd read detective or true crime books we wouldn't have crossed paths with Scarlotti. Then we wouldn't be getting all this healthy sun and exercise that my doctor suggested.

JACK

All right, So I'm stupid. Let's save our energy to get to those hills.

WE CALL IT GRACE

Somehow you seem to doubt your value
You define yourself as "damaged goods".
But is we are … are not we all…
With our coulds, our can'ts , our shoulds.

If we did not have our human side,
If we all had not slipped and fell,
We'd have carried our cross with Jesus
Up that scull shaped foreign hill.

Are we ever damaged beyond repair?
Can we make that fateful call
To condemn ourselves for bygone acts
Be they large or be they small.

The right to judge is but for Him
Who paid with blood that awful price
Who as our God was lifted up
In His death called "The Sacrifice."

Forgive yourself, for He does forgive
Our sins when He's called upon.
He asks us just to ask of him.
Our sins to purge and calm.

Only that which we have done ourselves
Can tilt the scales that weigh us down.
The acts of others bring us no guilt
To win or lose the crown.

So if you think you're damaged goods
It matters not what you've done
An act of Christ has made it naught
And a victory has been won.
04/16/2012

WHAT IS LIFE

What is this thing called life
    That the youth are looking for?
        Are they really looking for it
            Or avoiding it. What's in store?
Life sometimes is not the great jewel
    That those who look are seeking;
        But actually it is an elusive form
            And the way it's going, anything.
My life finds realism in trial.
    Life is but a trial of trials
        That one must pass or fail
            As one walks on mile after mile.
This life is a nice journey,
    If you but choose the way
        That will bring you greatest happiness
            At the end of the day.
And these choices aren't all easy
    And the way is often very rough,
        But I'm sure we can make it
            If we sweat and strain enough.
And when this day is over
    What then? Do you know that?
        What lies beyond the great curve
            Around which you cannot come back?
Does it matter, really truly matter?
    What is for me and you after?
        Is it important to see the end
            If it's of tears or of laughter.
All I can do is my best.
    All I can give is my all.
        That when I go from this life
            I can stand strait and tall.
I must be the honest kind,
    That life be found not of lies,
        That truth can be of life
            And not be found a surprise.
That this life can be full of joy
    And all that which accompanies it.
        That I might know of all the lives
            I have sought, and found, and lived it.

1970

What's Hidden There?

After a while this gets to be more of a repetitive art than what looks like a routine task.
It's your attention to detail and powers of observation you use to thwart the Inmate's mind.
Just entering the cell when it's empty you're putting yourself at risk 'cause you're in his world.
It may be ten by fourteen, concrete walled, with bed and commode bolted to the wall
But he has nothing to do for eighteen hours a day than to sit alone thinking of ways.
Ways to get out. Ways to hide hidden things to cut your throat or the throat of his enemies.
You have to use the system that works for you, left to right, top to bottom, reverse it each cell.
The towels hanging from the hook there...Is something folded in the cloth?... Is fabric missing being made into a rope?
The seams in every corner, nook and cranny...Have they been dug away and resealed with toothpaste to hide needles or shivs.
Has the stitching on the pillow or mattress been undone to hide things that make blood in the night?
Are things pasted to the bottom of the desk or chair with toothpaste, which is used like home owners use duct tape?
Have you ever lain on the floor and looked up at the bottom of the fixtures in your bathroom?
There are pockets and gaps in the castings that would make a paranoid cop cringe in wonder.
You use a mirror to check each point, because they might leave a dirty needle as a booby trap.
HIV and hepatitis are as deadly as any Pungi stick left in the jungle for you by Charlie Cong.
You never forget to check the pipes and collars that carry water to and the waste from a fixture.

Have they been used or pulled apart to hide the things he doesn't want you to find.
Has a toothbrush handle or a spoon been honed by dragging it across the smooth concrete floor?
Has a paperclip been sharpened into an icepick-like point that could send you to the hospital?
An old magazine carefully soaked and rolled and dried to a hard-packed rod that can crush you like a bat.
Has a bar of soap been sawn open by the back and forth motion of a single piece of thread
Then hollowed out to conceal anything you can imagine then it is smoothed and sealed with a wet finger.
After all these years working with these demented minds of the crook I think I'm getting that way too.
I feel hard pressed to trust anyone who doesn't also were a badge and shares the burden of it.
Maybe this is how we feel and think as we place them in that cell and slam the door.
To keep his warped mind occupied with its devious twists in jail and not out there
Where he would be hurting you and taking your property to support his accustomed lifestyle.
Be that a cheep hotel with weekly rates or a camp on the river where he pollutes our water too.

09-23-99

WE'LL MISS DIANE

Willingly the poet would crush his quill
Rather than pen this poem of woe.
A poem of a fair Juliet, of an Ophelia
Stilled by their own hands long ago.
Another heart is stilled that warmed ours,
That we called friend, and perchanced to love.
And cherish that we had the chance
Ere she fled to that promised land above.
Oft times we talked, exchanged a barb
Or word of hope, or a proffered hand
To ease the journey 'cross life's little hills
And to steady ones feet upon life's sand.
We'll miss her voice, her knowing smile,
Her wit, her sarcasm, and her loving ways,
The time she took with each of us
Brightening moments, and hours, and days.
And now she's gone. Driven from us
With the suddenness of a summer storm
Vanishing over the horizon leaving little sign
That from us she was untimely torn.
We stand in shock from the sudden loss.
Numb in disbelief that she is no longer here.
Expecting to see her around the next corner
And yet sensing that she's still very near.
We come to bid her one last goodbye
To heal our hearts in some small way
Admitting to ourselves that the sun has set
Ending her short, yet beautiful, day.
We've all sat in the calm of night,
After the days cares have passed away.
So now we sit and miss her smile,
Pondering, Questioning, But not judging today.
We'll all miss Diane. She leaves an empty space
In our souls, and surely in our hearts,
And our tears seek to wash away the pain,
As she, who chose too soon, departs.

09-24-97

WHAT I WAS DEALT

If I was at Hogwarts
I would see Thestrals,
Their wings of leather spread,
Bodies rising as its wings fall
I've seen too much death.
I've seen pain of torn limbs,
Of bones pushed past point of breaking,
Of darkness as the Devil grins.
It wasn't a wave of wands
But the clash of rushing metal
Driven by engines of hot iron,
Pushed far by weight on the petal.
Or driven hunks of heavy lead
Tearing flesh and spilling blood,
So precious, held warm deep inside
Flowing loose to make some mud.
Things I should not have seen,
Feeling I should not have felt,
Because I had a job to do.
It 's just the hand I was delt.

01-23-12

When Walking

When walking in the mountains
      I just happened to observe
That colors were put together
      To calm and soothe the nerve.
I turned and told my cousin
      On the trail close by
That God ---in His creations
      Has got an artist's eye.

I look at things of nature
      The flowers, the ferns, the trees
And their colors all work together,
      My senses they do please.
And not just with my optics
      Does this harmony disclose
But wafted in this gentle breeze
      Are scents that tease my nose.

Listen to the rustling trees,
      The twitter too of birds,
Like the work of a composer
      That the poet puts to words
And feel the coolness of the breeze
      And the coldness of the lake
Put here by a loving God
      A blessing for our sake.

06-09-2001

WHISTLE

Sometimes in the nighttime
I whistle to the moon
I share with him my muses
He hears my lonesome tune

My whistling bounds and echoes
Off the rocks and off the hills
Sending music madly spinning
Doing loops and twirls and spills

My whistling, like my verses
Brings solace to my heart
For they both are types of music
Running scales and doing parts

Parts of music of the master
That were written for a King
Then others of the common folk
To hum, to strum, to sing

That I whistle over and over
To please old man moon and I
As I sit and breathe the night air
As he marches 'cross the sky.

6-17-99

WINTERS ADIEU

The winds blow hard
And the clouds move
Down the western mountains

My freshly mowed lawn
rustles in the wind
Sporting its buzz cut.

Soon an April rain
Will dampen my grass
Saving me some water

And Peavine gets snow.
It's dusted with white
Like an elder's hair.

Nevada's spring is fickle
Warm, cold, then warm,
Screwing with the buds

Freezing off the petals
Of every flowering tree
Killing off the fruit.

But days will warm.
Leaves will burst forth
As they always do.

Playing in the sun
Becomes each child's lot
As winter bids adieu.

04-18-2001

WRATH

I hate it.
I hate it!
I hate it!!!

I have a job where my work desk computer is being used 24/7 by any number of people. We have all received, at least, minimal training on the network and programs we use in these computers.
Then why does some scum sucking moron have to go into areas of the computer and make the computer useless?

Obviously someone has way too much time on his or her hands and doesn't mind screwing his or her fellow workers. Not only is this stupid because we can't get the job done as it needs to be done. But you really piss off your fellow worker. Fellow workers at my office all wear guns. We are trained and retrained on how to overcome and kill any opposition. Yet some fellow worker uses his or her time to remove drives from the directory, delete links, and delete information.

I went to work on Monday and I couldn't get into H: drive. That's where all my reports are stored. The super moron had played with the terminal and made completing a report impossible. Nor could I print out anything for the sergeant. I was completely frozen out of the drive. Right clicking on the icon and trying to re-establish the links didn't work because the computer had been told there was no H: drive. Checking with others I found out not one of them could get into their files. They had been going to other terminals to get work done.
I finally had to contact I.T. twice to get someone down into the secure area to work his magic. I use the term magic because the science he uses is so far above what I know I feel like a caveman.

If I find out for certain which of my co-workers did this deed I will make it equally difficult for him or her to use the computer keyboard when necessary because of the reinforced plaster of Paris casts covering both of his or her arms.

Beware the wrath of a pissed off pig.

10-23-2001

XXXXLY POETIC

Inversely Poetic
Reversely Poetic
Conversely Poetic
Transversely Poetic

Perversely Poetic
Diversely Poetic
Adversely Poetic
Subversively Poetic

Constantly Poetic
Redundantly Poetic
Covertly Poetic
Substantially Poetic

Importantly Poetic
Intuitively Poetic
Instinctively Poetic
Sexually Poetic

Titillatingly Poetic
Scintillatingly Poetic
Uniquely Poetic
Obliquely Poetic

Quintessentially Poetic
Forcibly Poetic
Destructively Poetic
Constructively Poetic

Undoubtedly Poetic
Ubiquitously Poetic
Disturbingly Poetic
Unsettlingly Poetic

Twistedly Poetic
Pervertedly Poetic
Enlightenedly Poetic
Decisively Poetic

Transitively Poetic
Permanently Poetic
Eternally Poetic
Poetically Poetic

Temporally Poetic
Spiritually Poetic
Humbly Poetic
Finally Poetic

03-21-2001

You can have your city

You write about your city streets
Tall buildings and the neon lights
And let me write of the mountains
And the stars that fill my nights.

You talk about the hood and gangs
And pavement beneath your tire
And I'll tell you of a coyotes song
And how sparks fly from the fire.

You show me stores and shopping malls
Where people push and rush and crowd
I'll show you how to pitch a tent
And only the thunder is loud.

When you walk, You watch behind back.
You see beggars, drunks, and thieves.
But I listen to the wind at night
As it nudges sage and trees.

You can have your city lights
And your caves of brick and steel
Just let me have my country life
Where the scenery is fresh and real.

02/21/2002

YOUR SMILE

I don't think you know what you do to me
With just that little smile and the sound of your voice.
You get everything that you ask of me.
It isn't like I had some kind of choice.

I was bound to that smile when I met you.
I wanted to be your friend but you ignored me.
It took months to get to know you
And from that time I haven't been free.

I see you now and you come up to me
And we talk a minute and exchange hellos
And a hug, and a peck on the cheek.
The fire that is within me grows.

But it isn't like I think you really care
I'm just another sugar daddy for you,
Another one trapped by just your smile,
That you will discard like an old shoe.

I guess I should know better
But I am used to being hurt.
With all I've had I've grown a callous
Right across my often wounded heart.

Come. Wound me again,
Let me bare again my breast
And give you leave to strike
For you will hit but emptiness.

01/06/2001

Your Wedding Day

Her hand in his,
His hand in hers,
And they become as one
With lumps of gold
Rolled out in rings
They shine like golden sun.
With words of faith
They troth their love.
They pledge a sharing heart
And vow a vow
To whom they love
That they will never part.
They now shall share
Their days and nights
And together they will grow
And they shall build
One life from twain
In ways they'll only know.
We wish them peace.
We wish them love.
We pray they will endure.
The quakes of life
That time will bring
That love alone makes sure.

A toast we raise
And bid them luck
In journeys through the years,
That's marked by beauty
And marked by time
And often stained with tears.
May each one strive
To spoil their mate
And do the other's will
And serve each other
As hand in hand
They each other's dreams fulfill
We see then off.
They set their sails
And cast their lines away.
They're on their own
Bound fast by love
On this their wedding day.

Made in the USA
Middletown, DE
02 April 2025

73559886R00138